INTRODUCTION

Writing this all down has taken so much from me.
Releasing these words, has been painful, enlightening, sorrowful,
uplifting,
Convicting and cleansing.

God has given me the ability to paint a picture in ways I couldn't
have guessed.
I know it is God, because it is not me.
The people who came in and out of my life, adding or detracting
(I thought), were but the parts of my story being woven together.

I fought to glean the things that were good and to become aware of
the power that good, bad and even evil had on me.
Doing the same things over and over was an unbreakable cycle.
I looked up to God and begged with a broken heart and a clear
knowledge of my worth.
I have no value without God.
I am a child of the King, with God.

The things I am guilty of have been pardoned, the things others have
done to me, I forgive.
Not by my power at all. Not by my will at all. Only by the Grace of
God and His great healing power. Because, I allowed Him to
minister to my wounds and make me aware of the wounds I have
inflected.

He has been patient with me. I have had to come back time after
time, when I have turned back or lost my faith. Living in this world
is a battle. I am bombarded with the opportunity to fall into sin.
Small things that have bigger things they lead me to. The only way
to be able to stay strong is to live in the light. Watch my company
and yet be able to share the way to the God of the ages to those in
the darkness.

PART 1

MY BEGINNING

It was a hot day
A June day
Most people were inside
out of the heat
enjoying something cold.

People's lives were just moving along
unaware of the things that were happening
all around them.

The day was like any other
The sun moving slowly across the sky
 a final flash of color then disappears,
evening at last.

The day passed by
people settled into their supper
then to a comfy chair.
Meanwhile,

An airman
21-years-old
with deep blue eyes
a dash of freckles
and dark hair
sat in the little bar
drinking beer.

He was wondering where he left his smokes.
While he was watching some women
dancing
by themselves
laughing.

He had no knowledge
and little interest that his 19-year-old wife
was barely holding on to life,

3

two streets over.
The young woman had been in labor for 10 hours.
She tried to find her husband
with no luck.

Finally, she took her 11-month-old son to her neighbor
walked slowly across base to the hospital.

Each step was considered,
drawing closer to the hospital,
closer to the end of another pregnancy.

She felt safer
when she stepped in the big doors.
The air conditioning was a godsend.

As she made her way
to the maternity ward she stopped
she rested one hand on her bulging belly
the other on the wall.

The next contraction passed.
When she looked up
she was at the nursery window.

Peering into a full room of babies.
She let out a slow breath and kept going.

The night nurse led her to a
doorway at the end of the hallway,
several beds in a row were her first sight.

Women in labor,
others who had given birth
lay regaining strength.
Some were waking up from the fog.

She put the gown on that the nurse
gave her.
Standing on shaky legs and
holding on to the bed frame
she made it through another pain.

The nurse that came to get her
after what seemed like hours,
was tall and all business.

This young woman who was very soon
to be the mother of two,
sat in a wheelchair to go into the surgery.

Her labor was harder,
she was trying to stay calm.
The nurse helped her onto the surgery table.
She couldn't believe she was just here
only11 months earlier.

Her water broke as soon as she laid down.
The nurse said, "Don't worry it's perfectly normal."

The anesthesia was given through a mask.
The smell was nauseating not pleasant at all.
She wanted to push it away,
but her hands held on to her taut belly.

"Ok Roberta can you count backwards from 100?"
She was looking at the nurse's hat as she started counting
"100, 99, 98, 97, 90" she was under.

Her wrists were strapped down with leather cuffs.
The contractions were strong and hard,
doing their work even better
since she was no longer fighting the pain.
Her breathing became shallow after 15 minutes

then her heart fluttered.
The flutters got less
and less.
The monitors slowed
there was no heartbeat left.

The baby was
moments from bursting forth
into the delivery room of
Malmstrom Air Force Base Surgery suite.

The sedation was stopped
only oxygen now,
to get her to wake up fast.

Labor had stopped.
She was slipping away.
The doctor didn't do an episiotomy
there was already tearing.

Out of her body now,
looking down
on this sad scene.

She just watched
unsure what was really happening.
Off in the distance
she thought she could hear singing.

She looked toward the sound.
Moving slowing toward a tunnel
just by wanting to.
This tunnel seemed to span this earthly realm
and the next.

The light was brighter than she had ever seen.

She was drawn to it with
questions and increasing joy.

"Roberta, come on you have to try"
"Please come back", the doctor was lightly slapping her face,
"Come on, this little one is going to need you"
"Get me the smelling salts"
the nurse moved quickly and handed the doctor the smelling salts.
He snapped it open and under her nose

The voices in the OR were getting more muffled.
She couldn't make sense of the words.

Suddenly, she felt the pull in both directions.
The want to go on and leave this life was strong.
While considering which,

she was snatched back from the light.

The pain was unbearable,
she heard screaming long and loud.
Opening her eyes to see who was screaming
she realized it was her.
She was pulling and twisting her arms
frantically trying to free herself.

"Thank God!"
The doctor grabbed the tiny baby
as it slid into the world,
she was quiet and still;
he hung her upside down
slapped her little bottom.

She finally cried weakly.

ONE IN ONE OUT

The Twilight sleep kept moms from
memory of the birth.
Although, bruised and sometimes bleeding wrists
were dark proof of the process.

If the delivery process was extended
it would allow the twilight drugs to cross
through the placenta
to the baby.

The morphine mixture was
too much for this little girl.
She took two days to be totally free of it.

The baby was birth #125
Malmstrom Air Force base in the year 1955.
Birthplace was noted as Cascade County,
Great Falls, Montana.

No time,
No weight or length
recorded.

Mother and baby,
both stayed in the hospital for 5 days.
Bedrest was ordered for both.

Five days later
her husband still
didn't show up.

She called her neighbor and finally got to go home.

The final bill would have been a whopping $94.00
they would make payments on that sum for a long time,
if they hadn't been in the Air Force.

She told me I was born
after she died,

that the first woman
ever to go to the electric chair
was on the day and time of my birth.

A Touching Story

I was born a cute little
very pale skinned girl
curly fly away reddish hair
big blue sparkling eyes
soft and pink full of coos and smiles.

She said I didn't like to be touched
so she didn't hold me
much.

My mother told me
a few weeks after I was born
she was craving apples.
She said I was very fussy
she couldn't seem to comfort me.

An angel showed up at the door
with two apples,
she asked my mom if she could hold me,
she did.

Mom said she laid down
took a nap
woke up to me sleeping,
the angel was gone.
She said she knew it was an angel
it was the dead of winter
there were no apples to be had anywhere.

Odd, I was born the first week of June.

I remember a picture of me
about a year old or so,
I was on the sidewalk
standing with my hands on a telephone pole,
smiling that wrinkled up nose grin,
included gums, that babies do.

I had my high-top baby shoes
white socks
flour sack dress.

There were bandages
wrapped all the way up my legs
disappearing under my dress.
This picture, frozen in time.
My brother had pushed my stroller
into the fire place
he was playing
didn't know it would
burn my legs badly

I wonder if that is really what happened?
I don't see any sign of it now.
I don't know if I saw a picture of the stroller
heard the story so many times,
I felt like I remembered it.
Maybe my mom took the picture.

I looked as full of wonder and curiosity as any little girl.
Learning to crawl and walk and pick things up.
The wonders were discovered at every turn.

Wonder lasted only two or at most three years.
When that was ripped away
by whom I'm told,
should be the most trusted person
in a little girl's life…….
my

father.

PRAYERS OF NO

I have flashes of memories of a poor little girl.
She was being terribly
hurt
in pain
somehow,
I didn't understand.

I can see her from my place
high up in the room
almost at the ceiling.

She was always afraid
afraid to go to sleep tonight.
She tried so hard to stay awake and vigil.
She counted the stipes on the wallpaper.
She sang songs.

She prayed
For help
Into the air she pleaded
No help came
No help, ever

Once again,
she was roused by him touching her.
She grabbed her panties.
He already was there, pulling.

No, she said,
just one time,

more from surprise than power.
She knew she could do nothing,
she didn't even cry.

She tried not to look
kept her mouth and eyes tightly closed.

There was loud screaming inside her head,
why couldn't anyone hear it,
it was deafening.

His soft voice said,
"let daddy see"

"No", it was a simple word.
A short word, it could be said 3 times fast so easy,
NO,No
no.

Nothing came out.
Anger built inside,

PAIN TO BEAR

I thought of doing bad terrible things.
She wouldn't let me.

I grew more and more indifferent to her
just like watching some dumb animal
something from a story maybe,
you know, made up
it couldn't possibly
be real.

I don't want to see anymore.

I went away for a long time.
I wanted to fly away and soar over mountains
to see fields of flowers,
I wanted to hear birds singing
happy safe people.
Please God, stop him.
I'm just a little girl.

She must have been very bad,
why would this happen to a good person?
These bad things would not happen to her
if she wasn't bad.
She didn't seem bad.

She would play through the day,
mostly singing
pretending all kinds of things.
Eat with the family,
take a bath.

Then, she would be afraid.

At first, she was only afraid at night,
bedtime.
It wasn't long until it didn't matter

what time
where she was,
who was there.

I hate the word Daddy.

MOMMA ARE YOU THERE?

Where is her momma,
why is she never there?
She tells me about all the fun we had
the good things she did for me.

I don't remember it at all.
She must be confused,
maybe she is remembering a story
could she be lying?

Why can I remember my father so clearly?

I have only brief flashes of my mom's angry face.

How did she never see him doing this to me?

There are a couple pictures of me
dressed up in cute dresses,
she would say "I made that dress"
She never said, "Look how cute you were"

I don't see pictures
of being hugged or kissed
or even smiled at,
could they tell I was bad?
Wonder why I can't remember that?
Do other kids remember these things?

EDGES AND ANGELS

I was disjointed
I tried to stay
for fear I would not come back.
Sometimes it was just easier
to go away.

I knew this was not normal.
It gave me another thing to hide.
This is probably not fixable,
I just have to keep it hidden.

I prayed every night –
It was more like a stern angry talking to,
To God,
I was mad!

What did I do God?
Why if you love little children
are you allowing this to happen to me?

I wish I had one of those guardian angels.
I look at that picture stuck on a nail over my bed.
It was tattered around the edges.
The angel was protecting the little children
as they crossed a bridge
in a terrible storm.
I looked at it again and realized,
they were still in the storm though.

That didn't seem like help.

How was I ever to figure this out?
I am tattered around the edges also.
The voice in my head tried to push me
to the edge of here and gone.
it was mean,
I had to tell it to be quiet, a lot.

A Memory

24

****

I remember,
I was at one time very small a child.
Funny I don't remember a lot of good about it.
I can remember being given a doll to play with.
I decided it was a he, and named him Alan,
after being told I had to give him a name.

Was the name to call him if he were lost
or to introduce him to people?
It wasn't like he was going to answer to it.
It felt just odd even stupid
to play like this plastic doll
was my baby.

I was sure
I must have something wrong with me,
other girls played with dolls and carried them around
pretended to feed them and change them.

I didn't want to pretend I had a baby

that was my worst nightmare.

Allen was naked.
I didn't want to touch him
I wrapped a towel around him.
I think my mom made him some clothes.
He probably came from a second-hand store or a neighbor.

The next Christmas I got a doll bed,
what a strange thing I thought,
do I now have to pretend he sleeps and be quiet?

Yes, there was definitively something wrong with me.

****

MOONBEAM MEMORY

Once at grandma's house I snuck through the house in the dark,
the sound of the floor creaks and pops seemed like loud giant's
footsteps
as I tried to take long steps skipping boards to get quietly to my
grandpa's chair.
There was just a sliver of light coming through the picture window,
it lit up grandpa's chair,
thank you moon.

I loved to sit in this place.
I leaned way back and crossed my legs up high.
This place smelled like him,
his pipe was there,
I would put it in my mouth and breathe it in.
I loved that cherry tobacco smell and taste.

I looked at the big bible on grandmother's end table,
it had beautiful color pictures of Jesus.
It was ok to turn the pages and look at it
as long as I was gentle, grandma said.

I so liked the one where he was surrounded by kids.
But, me – he just didn't like me I guess.
I know I wasn't pretty,
lots of freckles,
just not pretty at all,
plus, right here I sat

with a pipe in my mouth.

FARMING

Grandpa had a big farm.
He grew different things at different times.
The Farmer's Almanac would say when to plant stuff.
Like dark of the moon for stuff that grew in the ground.
Like potatoes and carrots, beets, turnips and onions too.
That always was a mystery to me.
The moon would make stuff grow?

He said you've got to rotate the crops.
One year we might have corn and another tobacco.
I liked the tobacco,
I liked corn too
but different.

Grandpa grew giant tobacco.

The fields were so tall, way over my head.
Only he knew when it was time to cut the tobacco.
He would go through the fields
feeling the leaves
smelling them.
He even felt the soil.

He said it had to be just moist enough.
Not too wet or too dry.

We would wait until the heat of the day was past.
When the day was right,
all of us would get in line and go down the rows.
Grandpa, Mama Lee, Papa Lee, Grandma, Mama, Dad, me and
Rudy.

I didn't cut the leaves, but I did get to carry them.
It took a long time to get through all the rows.

The stalks looked naked when we were done.
I remember one time we were down a row,

my mom screamed.
She ran from the field.

My heart was pounding,
I ran as hard and fast as my legs would take me,
to see what was wrong.
Everyone popped out of their row almost at the same time.
She had cut a leaf
there was a tobacco worm on it.

The worms are big and green with big eyes.
They looked like the inch worm on cartoons.

I thought it was funny, some of them laughed,
Grandpa just shook his head as he headed back down a row.
He shouted over his shoulder,
"Let's get this done before dark"
"I hope you killed that tabaca worm"

The tobacco leaves were wrapped in small bunches of a few leaves
then tied together with twine at the cut end.
The leaves hung up high in the barn.
As they swayed, the noise the leaves made almost sounded like wind
through the trees.

The whole inside of the ceiling of the barn was upside down leaves
waving in the breeze.
I remember Grandpa saying to make sure and leave room for the air
to circulate,
we didn't want them to mold.
He raised the bundles up with a long pole with a hook on the end.
That was the best smell ever.

I would lay on the hay pile and watch it sway back and forth while it
dried.

I didn't realize that this was what cigarettes were made from.

I did see my grandpa pull a little draw string bag out of his pocket,
pour some of the contents into a piece of paper
then roll it up and lick the side.

I just didn't realize that was tobacco for the longest time.

Tobacco smells good, cigarettes stink.

Sweet, Red dirt memories

We all sat out under the tree by the porch after the field was all cut.
Grandma and Mama Lee and Momma too, would go start supper.
Grandpa got the ice cream churn ready.
Grandma would bring the milky mix hot from the stove.
The vanilla scent was strong as she poured it in.
Grandpa would turn the churn
until he could tell the ice cream
was starting to freeze.

We got to take turns turning the handle then.
I liked to take little pieces of the ice
and put them in my mouth.
The rock salt was good to.
It was a hard job, but we knew it would be worth it.

Grandma would send me or Rudy under the house where she kept
her canning.
She would give directions where to go.
"Crawl past the first post, then go left,
the second bunch of jars is the black berries."

Sometimes we would crawl all the way out into the light
only to see it was a jar of green beans.
We would do it again; the berries were really good on the ice cream.
I wonder how the jars got here?
Did grandma crawl under the house?

The smell of the dirt under the house was like a perfume to me
it was cool even when it was hot outside.
I liked the red color it was.
Not everyplace has red dirt.

REALITY RETURNS

The good times were too few
my real life would be back.
I was sure people were laughing at me.

I always had a voice in my head
telling me I'm worthless.
I try to sing or whistle,
so, I can't hear it.

But I could hear it,
I could always hear the torment.

If anybody ever found out
I would be a Disgust,
that's what he told me,
no one would love me,
really how could they.
I was gross and dirty,

a Disgust that sounded awful.

I would never get use to this
being my life
forever.

How do people get to be grownups?
Will I be able to leave and take care of myself someday?

I am so afraid to be on my own.
I don't know what to do.
There was no way out,
ever.

Even if I told, I would be put in a bad place.
I was already in a bad place
stuck inside my head.

I was terrified
always terrified.

TRAIL ACROSS TENNESSEE

I remember we lived in a "partment" building.
We walked up a lot of stairs to our "partment".
It was dark inside.
Dark walls and dark wood floors.

I could lay on the floor at the heater vents
it was warm,
I could listen to the people below us.
It was fun to pretend they were my family.
They were usually happy and laughing.
Their food smelled good.

I got told to get myself up out of the floor,
sometimes many times a day.
I was just drawn back
over and over to the joy,
the mystery that filled downstairs.

I remember bringing home a picture
from somewhere,
school maybe.
I don't know how old I was.
It might have been vacation bible school.
I always liked that.

My Momma said she liked my picture.
I still can remember how big she smiled.
I don't remember what the picture was.
It didn't seem as important
as Momma's smile,
that was a good memory.

I think Momma kept my drawing on the mirror
there until we moved.

BLESSING OF ILLNESS

I was once again laying with my ear to the heater vent.
"Ty Beth get in here and eat your breakfast",
"Coming Momma"
I ran to the table for breakfast
happy and ready to eat.
It smelled so good,
pancakes and warm syrup.

Rudy was eating his breakfast.
His plate was almost empty already.
I was just about to take my first bite

My dad kicked my chair
and me in it
across the kitchen floor.

"I'm not eating looking at that!"
He pushed his chair back and it flipped over.
He tossed his napkin down and walked out.

I was tossed hard into the floor,
I still had my fork in my hand,
but the pancake was under the table.

Momma must have been shocked to,
she turned around with the spatula in her hand.
I think she yelled at him.

I got up and cried,
syrup was all over me even in my hair.
Momma wiped my face with the dish rag
She told me to eat and then she would give me a bath.
I ate but I didn't enjoy it at all.

Rudy was still eating like nothing happened.

I had Impetigo.

It was itchy and gross, but the cream stuff helped.
I was not supposed to scratch it
because momma said it would leave bad scars.
Momma said it came up through the heater vents,
carried by cat hair.
When she told me that,
I thought with a smile,
the neighbors have a cat.

I had to have this yellow cream stuff put on my face,
it stunk really bad,
Momma said it smelled like rotten eggs.

I didn't get to go anywhere until I was all healed up.
I got to listen to the neighbors
look out the window
draw pictures on brown paper bags.

I went all kinds of places in my head.
I was happy to have the yellow stuff on my face
it was a little sad when I got all better.

Dad didn't want to get near me
that whole time I had the stuff on my face.

Sweetwater

I think it was 1959.
We lived in Sweetwater, Tennessee
Momma said it must have had good water.

We next lived in a place where we had a neighbor lady
that had the polio.
I thought that meant the poles she walked with.
It wasn't.

She had to walk with crutches,
they weren't broken leg crutches.
They had arm rests and a cuff at the wrist.
She let me put my hands into the handles,
but they were too tall for me.
We would sit out on the stoop
where it was not so hot.
We sat out there most evenings.

She let me brush her hair sometimes
her hair was very long and black.

She would brush mine to.
I liked this time very much.
One of her legs was tiny like mine almost,
but she was a grown-up lady.

Her shoes were different sizes.
She said she had to buy two pairs when she got shoes,
but, she only had one pair.

I remember her name was unusual to me, Maria Paloma.
She said it meant "dove".
She told me I was uncommonly smart
for such a young child.
That made me wonder, why that was.

I heard my Momma telling her

she had to keep my brother Rudy
in a drawer in the closet.

Because my dad would beat him if he cried.
She said he beat him one time until he quit crying.

Was she home when this happened?

She would have stopped him, if she had been there.

How would she know what had happened?
if she wasn't there.

She took him to the hospital
he was hurt bad
the beating had caused him to have a rupture.

I don't think I remember that,
I guess I wasn't here yet.

I think this is where my little brother was born.

BABY RANDY

This new baby was going to be my little brother Randy.
Of course, we didn't know it
until momma went to the hospital though.

It was November 1960 when he was born.
Randy was very cute.
Momma had to hold Randy a lot,
he was sick and wouldn't sleep.

She gave him camphor with some sugar.
She would blow in his face
then pour it in his mouth.
Me and Rudy hated the crying.
When he was starting to crawl around,
he fell over a lot.

His head was swollen, squishy and lopsided.

Randy was sick and had to go to the doctor.
The doctor sent him straight to the hospital.

My momma said his head was full of water.
The doctor had to put needles in his head
to let out the water.
I think he was fine after that.

I kept my head out of the water just in case.
I sure didn't want to get needles in my head.

When we went to get my brother from the hospital finally,
he was happy to see us,
his eyes were all red it looked like he had been crying.
I hugged him.

There was a little girl there that drank something
that burned her throat till it was gone.

She had a bandage around her neck with a tube coming out.
Momma said that was for her to breathe.
The doctor put a lid on her side
they could put food in.
Momma said her food went right to her stomach.
She said the little girl would never taste food again.
She was also unable to talk
because of the damage in her mouth.
She smiled at me though.

Will she be better?
No one would tell me if she would be better.

What did she drink?

Bottom drops with a snap..

48

The next place I remember living was Strawberry Plains,
that's in Tennessee also.
This was 1961, I think.
We had a dog,
Blue was her name.
She was a Weimaraner,
she was gray, Momma said she was blue though.

We didn't have a fence around our yard here.
Blue would sit with her bottom on the step
her front feet on the ground
wait until Randy was almost to the end of the yard
then she would trot out and pick him up by his diaper
carry him back to the step and drop him.
It made Randy screaming mad.
It was funny to watch.

My Dad worked in a milk delivery truck.
He didn't get to deliver to our house,
he had a different route Momma said.

Our milk man would drive up in his white milk truck
Randy would say, "choca milt, choca milt!"
Sometimes we would get it and sometimes not.
The man always waited for momma to shake her head.
Me and Rudy would watch her too.

This is where I went to school for the first time.
Momma had made me underwear,
a slip with lace on it and a dress too.
I remember I felt very special and fancy.

When I got to school, I was shy.
It was very scary to me to be in this place where I didn't know
anyone.
I looked at the walls, the floors, the lights and the people.
I always noticed things

like if someone was missing a finger or had a fake leg
or even if they buttoned their shirt wrong.
I would remember all the details.

I was shown where my desk was.
It even had my name written on a paper.
I traced it with my finger.
There was a tablet with lines for writing
a big fat black pencil
but mostly the brand-new crayons.
They smelled good and they were perfect,
I wanted to write or draw,
the teacher said we weren't supposed to do that yet.

I began to realize I needed to pee.
I almost waited until it was too late.
I was so afraid to ask to go.
The teacher pointed me in the direction of the bathrooms.
I walked down the hallway and let myself into the bathroom.
There was a glass in the top of the door,
but you couldn't see through it.

It was bright and clean,
I put my hand on the tile wall
It was cool and so smooth
but I wanted to get out of there
as fast as I could.

When I stood up my panties caught on the seat
and broke the elastic.
I was so panicked I didn't know what to do.
I walked back and forth in the bathroom
trying to figure out what to do.
I had to walk with my elbows tight against my sides
desperately trying to hold them up.
I was trying not to throw up.
When I got back to my class

I went right to my desk and sat down.

The teacher was telling everyone to come up
and get a musical instrument
to play like we were a marching band.
Everyone was excited and trying to get their favorite.
They started to march in a circle around the room.
They beat on drums, played the triangle, blew on flutes, even
chimes.
The teacher asked me to come and get an instrument.
I shook my head no and stayed in my seat.
She came to my seat
made me get up and join in the parade.
The only thing left was cymbals.
I tried to keep my elbows tight at my sides
to keep my drooping panties up.

It must have looked odd to the teacher,
the way I was playing the cymbals.
She came over and took my hands,
she pulled them wide apart -
down went my panties.

I dropped the cymbals
pulled them up and ran out of the class.
I don't think she noticed
she didn't say anything.
I went down the hallway and outside,
I was trying not to cry,

I didn't want someone to try to help me.

The bell rang, and kids came running out the door to the playground.
I had to keep my panties up with my elbows the rest of the school
day.
My arms and shoulders were hurting from squeezing so hard.
I was so relieved to go home finally.

I walked up the final two steps
into the safety of home.

When I got into the house I started crying.
Momma said, "didn't you like school?"
I told her about my panties,
she started laughing
I cried all the harder.

I was so careful after that
I checked my clothes to make sure they were clean,
hole free and the elastic was sewed in good.
I became oddly attached to my clothes.
I didn't think it was funny at all.

DARKNESS COMES TO LIGHT

My brother and I were getting ready for school one morning
we heard a commotion in the kitchen.

Momma and Daddy were talking in a loud whisper.
We each had an ear on the door trying to hear.
Dad was just getting home,
it was 7 in the morning.
They were arguing,
we couldn't tell what they were saying.
Then my dad's voice boomed,
if anyone asks - I was home all night
do you hear me?
Momma never answered him.

It was only a few minutes after that,
someone knocked on our door.
Mamma stood there for a second or two
she must have considered not answering it,

she answered it, Good morning Mr. Hedgecock
He didn't answer he just asked her if Jim was home.
Yes, she said.
Has he been here all night?

"Yes, he's been home all night, why?"
Mr. Hedgecock turned around
slapped his daughter real hard.
Then he pulled off his belt.

Momma said, what is wrong?
What has happened?

Annie said Jim raped her last night
She came home with her dress all ripped up.
It was probably that no-account boy whose been coming around

Mr. Hedgecock said he was sorry to bother her.

She shut the door and burst into tears,
we had opened our door and stood looking up at her.

Get in here and eat your breakfast before your late for school,
she wiped her face and got a cigarette.
It took years for me to understand what all this meant.
Momma must have been eaten up
with guilt over this,
right?

She would say how awful it was
about poor little Annie Hedgecock
out of the blue sometimes
when she was remembering those days.

What would I do if this was me?

I don't know.
We moved from there
I was just about to be in 1st grade.

I kept my crayons.

PAPER WISHES

56

We lived in a big city next
It was Chattanooga, Tennessee

We lived in a small room under some stairs for a while.
It even had a tiny door.
Not even tall enough for Momma or Dad to walk through
without stooping over.

Dad wasn't working so he was always home.
Momma was home too.
She did laundry and mending for people in the building.
We had a small window we could look out.
You could see people walking down the sidewalk
cars going by too.

We had a bunch of magazines and the Sears and Roebucks catalogs.
Mom said we should cut out pictures of what we'd like for
Christmas
and put them on the little Christmas tree just for fun.

We had made some paper chains for it,
but we didn't have any other decorations.
We cut out all sorts of things.
I remember cutting out a little easel
I thought it would be fun to paint.
I don't remember anything else I put on the tree.
The boys did it too
we all decided to cut out a dress for Momma and shoes too.
We were not used to getting anything much for Christmas.
We would get a stocking with nuts and an apple or an orange
a few pieces of hard candy or sometimes chocolate.

We were always happy with the stocking and occasionally a toy.

This year we woke up to all the things that we had hung on the tree.

We were screaming and jumping up and down.
We had never seen anything like it.

Even the dress and shoes for Momma.
I'm sure there was something for our Dad
I don't recall what it was.
Momma was crying.

One of the ladies in the building
Momma sewed for and did laundry
had seen our tree when she came to pick up her laundry and
mending.

I ask my Mom about this when I had kids of my own.
She said the lady upstairs and other neighbors had got together
and made all our Christmas wishes come true.

HIT OF A MISS

We didn't ever have a Christmas like that again.
It would stay a very special magical memory.

My dad sent me across the street to the store to get some 'cookies?'
I asked for the money,
he said it was already taken care of.

So off I went--maybe 6 years old—
I looked both ways and crossed the street.
I walked into this little store a bell that tinkled
when the door opened.
The hardwood floors,
squeaked when I walked around.
I walked up to the counter and told the man,

"I'm here to get the cookies for my Dad."
"Oh, Ok."
He seemed nervous or something,
my little radar was going off.

He walked to the end of the counter,
He stepped around the corner to the end,
"They're back here."
I stood there.
What was wrong here?
Again, he said, "They're back here.
"Do you want them or not?"

I put one foot in front of the other,
I still remember the squeak each plank on that floor made.
When I got to the doorway, he stepped inside and turned to me.
I took one step and saw a bed.

It took me a long moment to understand what was happening.

My Dad had sold me to the store man for a box of cookies!
I was screaming inside, and my little voice was
screaming run RUN!
So, I ran right out the door, and into the street.

By the time I heard the car horn it was too late.

I ran right into a car.
I got thrown to the curb.
I was very confused,
I couldn't figure out what had happened.

There were people looking at me all over the place.
I was embarrassed.
My wrists hurt,
I had a hard time getting up.
Someone called an ambulance,
I could hear the siren.

I had to be taken to the hospital in an ambulance,
it was a total blur.
They made me stay overnight.
I remember getting a giant Baby Ruth candy bar
when momma picked me up from the hospital.

I didn't feel like eating a candy bar,
I gave it to Rudy and Randy.
It was a whole day later when I got back to the house,
through the little door
under the stairs.
I went straight to my bed
backed up as far as I could
with my back to the wall.

My Dad was just sitting there.
He didn't say a word.

He didn't ask where the cookies were,
or if I had been in the man's bedroom.
Did the car kill me?
Nothing!

I was in the newspaper the next day,
"Girl hits car"
Momma and Daddy laughed when they read it.
I didn't think it was funny at all.

DID MOMMA CALL?

We had moved into a rooming house.
We were in a room with a table, a couple chairs
and a light bulb hanging from a cord.

We had to go down the hall to the bathroom.
We had pallets on the floor to sleep.
I would put what clothes I had under my head
we didn't have a pillow.

We were cold in this place,
Momma said the super wouldn't give us heat
for what we were paying.
She would heat up water on the hot plate
we got washrag baths.
We ate, a lot of macaroni and rice.
Sometimes Momma would bring home pie from the diner.

We only had one bed and my Dad was in it most of the time.
He took medicine with a needle.
Momma said. never touch his medicine.
I didn't, I hate needles.

We woke early in the morning.
We heard a knock on the door,
we weren't supposed to answer it.

"It's Grandpa", he said.
We all ran to the door.
He just looked down at us and smiled.

He said, "Where's your Daddy?"
I pointed to the sheet that hung over the bedroom area.
Grandpa went under the sheet and then pretty much right back out.

He came to pick us up while Momma was at work at the diner.
Dad was asleep, and Grandpa couldn't wake him up I guess.

He had us gather our clothes into a little suitcase.

We did,
he picked up Randy,
me and Rudy followed him to the car.
The car was so warm,
we slept all the way to Tellico Plains, Tennessee.
I was worried momma would be mad when she got home.
We didn't even leave a note.

We kept asking about Momma
did she know where we were.
Did she call you Grandpa? Grandpa never answered.

We started down their road and I felt excited.
It was always fun here
we were warm
we had good food too.

When we got there, it wasn't the same.
When we had come to visit before
it was happy.
Before, when we would run in,
they would be glad to see us.

I think they were glad to see us?

This time we all stood in the doorway
I was holding the suitcase.

Grandpa hung his hat on a hook on the porch.
He came and stood behind us.

"Did you see him?" she asked.
Grandpa just nodded and walked over to get some coffee.
I got a chill
Grandma seemed mad.

Our stomachs were growling loudly.
She shook her head as she looked down at each of us.

I looked around the room past her, it was very tidy.
They had built a new room and a bathroom in the house to.

She looked at each of us and shook her head again.

Grandma said we were to call her "Eva".

She started walking to the back of the house,
she didn't even look back
she just said,
"Come on".
Rudy said,
"Grandma, I have to pee".

She turned around let out a long breath and said,
"I said, call me Eva".
We tried,
but mostly we called her Grandma.

TOO MUCH TROUBLE...

We got settled in and started a routine.

Church on Sundays to start each week off.
My Aunt Patricia, pin curled my hair one Saturday night
for church the next day.

I dreamed I was getting bit all over by lizards.
It was all the bobby pins that had come loose,
they were all over the bed.

I never had her curl my hair again.
She thought it was pretty funny.
Grandma said my hair was too much trouble,
she cut it short.
I had really liked my hair.

A NEW NUMBER...

Rudy and I sang in church a lot.
Grandma had us sing, "Beneath the Cross of Jesus" and "The Old Rugged Cross"
She would make us practice at home, while she played the piano.

This one Sunday, Rudy said "let's sing a different song."
I looked at him, I shrugged my shoulders and he started singing,
I joined right in with him and we sang it loud too.
The ladies in the front pew were laughing into their hankies.
We saw how much they liked it, so we sang 3 verses.
Turns out,
"What shall we do with the drunken sailor"
isn't a church song.

We got a good talking to on the way home.
Grandpa did swat Rudy with his belt when got home.
I think Grandma told him to

Generation of memory

I don't know for sure how long we were there.
We ate and played
took baths
brushed our teeth, day after day.

We spent a lot of time 'catch'n lit'nen' bugs.

There were these big bug shells stuck to the trunk of the 'weep'n
wella' tree they were neat. Grandpa said the bugs crawled right out
of their skin and left it behind.
Can you leave your life behind like that too?
We would go inside when Grandma said lunch was ready
then we had to lay down for a little bit after we ate.
Then we were back outside till it was time for supper.

The sight of the 'lit'nen' bugs flying all around was so exciting.
We would sit on the edge of the hill in the lawn,
and wait for the 'lit'nen' bugs to start to float slowly toward us
like Tinkerbell they fluttered around.
I knew if I looked closer, I could see their fairy costumes
the fairy dust that sprinkled as they flew.
We would catch some in a jar.

Grandpa said we had to let them go before we went inside,
because they will die in the jar.
I surely didn't want the fairies to die.

We rolled down the grassy hills and got chigger bite.
Great Grandma, Mama Lee put rubbin alcohol on 'em.
Grandma just said, I told you not to roll in the grass.
We got to watch The Ed Sullivan show on Sunday nights
I always loved the mouse, Topo Gejo.

Great Great Grandpa, Papa Lee's father was about to have a birthday
we got to go see him.
The whole family drove to see our Great Great Grandfather.

72

Aunt Patricia didn't want to go, so she stayed home with Rudy and Randy.
They didn't want to go on a long hot car ride.

The drive was only a couple hours away, I think.
We pulled up this red dirt road,
I saw little shacks and Teepees, lots of them.
The sign said, Qualla Boundary Reservation.
He lived on a reservation?
There were a lot of Indians there.

Great Great Grandfather was Cherokee.
There was also Chickasaw Indians around us.
I didn't know which was which they seemed the same to me.
Papa Lee was telling me about the reservation,
he said they could hunt and fish when they wanted to.
They were a nation of their own.

We walked across a dusty field
where kids sat in the dirt with other kids
playing some sort of a game,
a dog was chasing his tail
some young guys were working on a car.
The car looked way out of place here.
When we reached a big teepee, we stopped.
Papa Lee said wait here.

He pulled back the cover over the doorway and ducked into the opening.
I looked closer at the cover over the door and I saw claws on it.
Grandpa said, "it is probably the last bear he'll ever hunt."
Papa Lee said something very quiet to his father.
He turned around and told us to come inside.

Grandpa and Papa Lee both took off their hats
the top of their heads was white where their hats covered.
I guess they kept it out of the sun.

Great Great Grandfather was mostly laying on a pile Indian blankets and a fur to.
His eyes were white.
He had feathers braided into his hair here and there.
Next to him was a wooden kitchen chair, it had a cup of something on it.
It smelled like tobacco in here.

Great Great Grand Father. said call him "Papa".
I ask papa how long he has lived in a tent?
He was very wrinkled, when he smiled he was even more wrinkled,
He laughed.
Papa Lee talked to Papa up close and touched his face.
Papa had some tears falling down.
I wasn't sure what to do.
They were happy and sad tears.

He said he had lived here a long time.
He told the story of his people and their suffering on the Trail of Tears,
then part of the people stayed in this place
part went to a reservation in Oklahoma.
Papa talked about the terrible walk that took so many lives.
He said he could never live in the white man's world.
I wondered if we lived in the white man's world or if it was somewhere else.
Papa talked to the ladies sitting with us.
I could not understand his words,
but they sounded neat.
The ladies got up and left us.
They had beads on their dresses in pretty designs.
These ladies had deer skin dresses the sleeves went do to about the middle of their forearm.
These older ladies that dressed like this, Mama Lee said,
had family that walked the trail of Tears.

Papa said the Cherokee had been here from the beginning.

He said this Tennessee was named after, Tanasi.
Tanasi was a Cherokee village, it became Tennessee June 1, 1796
when it became the 16th of the United States.

Many of the people we passed, had on clothes like ours but had a
beaded collar,
a medicine bag or feathers in their long hair.
Mama Lee said it was against the law for anybody that wasn't a
Cherokee
to have Eagle feathers or even Hawk feathers.
Papa leaned over and sipped from his cup and then he laid back on
his fur again.
He was looking pretty tired, so Papa Lee said we should go.

Papa gave me a pack of Juicy Fruit gum, he touched my face very
softly,
even though his hands were very rough, it didn't scare me.
Then he put his hand on my hair.
He said, "where are your braids little one?"
I didn't mind his touch at all it felt like love.

Mama Lee said he was almost blind,
but the old chief at 103 was doing pretty good.
We all got up and each went by to kiss Papa goodbye.
We walked out of the tent and into the bright sunshine.
The glare took a minute to get used to.
When I could see again, I walked toward the smell of the stew pot.
The ladies were cooking in a big black pot about the size
that grandma did washing in.
It smelled so good.

They started to scoop out bowls full.
I ask Grandma Eva if I could have some,
"No! we will eat when we get home"
I was persistent, "Grandma please"

She didn't answer she just looked at me, that was enough.

We got back in the car and I asked why she wouldn't let me have some?

"They were cooking puppies"
My mouth hung open.
I thought about it all the way home.
Great Great Grandfather was a Cherokee Chief, who ate puppies.

I wonder where he got the gum?

CANNING, COOKING & THE SEARS & ROEBUCKS CATALOG

"Mama Lee lived down the road about a mile from Grandma's house.
Papa Lee too.
They are our great grandparents.
We got to go over to Mama Lee's a lot.
Usually one or two at a time.

I got to go by myself usually.
I loved her house.
I remember my mom giving Mama Lee a small white box one day.
She opened it and took out a bible with color pictures on the cover and on the inside too.
I loved it.

I looked up at Mama Lee and said, "Mama Lee can I have it when you die?"
My mom said, "Ty Beth!" and looked at me like I had done something really bad.
Mama Lee patted me on the head and said, "She's ok, she didn't mean any harm"
"Sure, you can have it" She smiled at me, momma didn't smile.
That bible was right on the table all the time. She didn't like for us to touch it.
She said it was just to look at, no touching.

Momma Lee cooked on a big black stove, it looked like what trains were made of.
She had to put wood in it just like you do for the fireplace.
It also had a big place on the side that you fill with water and it makes hot water.
We got up when the sun got up and we went to bed when the sun went to bed.
Papa Lee was always up before the sun.
He would have been out and milked the cows
and feed horses, cows, and sometimes chickens too.
He would be back in washed up and hungry for breakfast.
He would sit in a big rocker by the fire every morning

while Mama Lee made breakfast.

Mama Lee made me breakfast,
we had cream of wheat with butter and brown sugar, and raisins.
Papa Lee always poured a little milk in it and tore up his toast in it to.
So,
I did mine that way.

His coffee smelled good, but I didn't like the taste.
Mama Lee made coffee gravy for the grits sometimes
I liked that pretty good.

She kept canned tomato juice in the sitting room closet.
She had to put a part of a match book folded in half tucked into the twisty lock,
so it would hold.
I remember the first time I saw the tomato juice
I didn't think I would like it.
She told me to try one small sip, I did
I liked it a lot. I never ever tasted tomato juice that tasted so good.
She canned a lot of tomato juice because she grew so many tomatoes
and didn't want to waste them.

The closet had all kinds of jars.
Big jars with berries and small jars with jelly.
Green beans, carrots, beets, corn and even potatoes.
She kept the cough drops in there too.
They were in a small tin box called "Sucrets".
She always said these are not candy.
She had this thing you put in your nose too.
When your nose was stopped up it would make you breathe good,
she said you shouldn't use it a lot or you might get hooked on it.

We had covers on our laps, so we would stay warm.
We would rock and eat; Papa Lee would spit in the fire.

The spit would sizzle and pop around on the hearth until it was all gone.
I always told him to do it again, and he would.
He would sit and have more coffee and smoke a cigarette
before he went back out to tend to the farm.

After breakfast, Mama Lee would go out to the outhouse with me.
I was afraid of the lizards and falling down the hole.
We would sit there in the two-seater and look through the Sears and Roebucks catalog.
Mama Lee said, "the best paper is the index pages, its softer"
"Don't even try to use the shiny pages unless that's all there is"
"If you keep the door open just a bit you can see better and get some air too.

I had so much to learn.

THE CHIEF AND THE CHEF

We would go gather eggs and fill up the
chicken's water most mornings after that.
I was afraid to reach under the chickens.
I would be all nervous and scared

Mama Lee just stuck her hand right under them chickens
they would go to squak'n and
she would just shhhsh'em.

One day she picked up a chicken and looked at it real close,
she ran here hand through the feathers
then picked up another one and did the same thing.

She put it down and said, "they have mites"
"Let's go get them the cure"
We went to the tool shed and got a black glass bottle.
I leaned my arms on the counter and watched her.

Mama Lee measured some into the chicken water,
"it turned the water kind of purple Mama Lee".
 "The chickens didn't care", she said,
"they know it will help 'em"

We would go down to the smoke house most every day
she would cut off some pork back
to put into her beans or get
some other meat for supper.
It smelled so good in there.

They kept it dark in there they kept it cool too.
Sometimes we would go
down to the spring and get watercress.
I would just pull some out and eat it.
It was crunchy and had a radish flavor to me.
Mama Lee said she didn't think so.

The spring was just down the hill behind the smokehouse.

It was shaded by a big tree.
I would wade my feet in.
It wasn't deep, but it would come up to my knee in some places.

I liked when we would go out to the
thicket way back past the fence and pick berries.
You had to get in there to get the berries,
it was really stickery so you had to be careful.

Mama Lee always said, "Ty Beth watch out for snakes"
I would back up and be real cautious
for a minute then right back in there again.
She usually had to tell me a bunch of times.

Then she would say, "Geezalou, child
you just get off in your own world"
She shook her head and laughed.

She would give us both a bowl of black berries
with sugar on them when we got back to the kitchen.

I was looking at my hands,
they were black from pick'n,
she said, "Don't fret, when we do up the supper dishes
your hands will be pink again"
She was right.

Mama Lee told me to go sit with Papa
while she got some more firewood.
I skipped across the back porch and in the door,

Papa Lee had pulled out some pictures
that night after the dishes were done and put away.
They were turkeys, I thought.
He said they were chickens.

The pictures were from the Indian Fair,

they were blue ribbon chickens.
Papa Lee said his father was a Cherokee chief
and he would have been one too.

Mama Lee was part Cherokee too.
"You mean Papa, right?" He nodded his head yes.
I wondered why Mama and Papa Lee
didn't live on the reservation?
I liked their house, so I was glad they didn't.

I found out they had to go to a different fair
because they were Indians.
"Why?" I asked.
He just closed the box of pictures
and tied the string around it.
Mama Lee had come in with an arm load of wood,
she laid it on the pile.
She wiped her hands on her apron
then patted Papa Lee on the shoulder,
she took the box from him and
put it up on the shelf where the Tomato juice was.

"Why did you put the pictures in the canning closet Mama Lee?"
"It's dark and good'n cool in there
that's good for both canning and pictures"

I went into the sewing room
which was also where the big feather bed I slept in was.
Mama Lee had a sewing machine that you sort of peddle.
In one of the small drawers
on the side there were some plastic beads.
It was a necklace I think,

I could pop them apart and put them back together.
I love the pop they made.
Mama Lee from the sitting room said.

"them beads are going to stop staying together if you don't stop that"
I popped them together one last time and put them back in the drawer.

"Mama Lee can we play the Victrola tonight?"
"We'll see"
That usually meant yes.
I pretty much didn't want to
go back to Grandmas until Saturdays –
She had TV and Cartoons.

COWS AND A CANDY BAR

Early one morning I heard a bunch of bells tinkling
I knew it was the peddler truck
coming up the road.

I loved to see the peddler truck coming up the road.
Mama Lee said he came out about ones'ta month.
The Peddler truck was a great big Red house on a truck.
He had bells hanging off the house.
He said it was to scare cows out of the way.
The man would honk as he came around the turn on their road.
He'd wave when he got out of the truck.

"Hello Luther", he said. Papa would shake his hand.
He would go to the back of the truck,
where he lifted down a set of steps.
We could climb up the steps
to walk around in the back of the truck.

I wondered what it would be like
to drive around
see all kinds of people
sell them candy and stuff.

I wonder if he could sleep back here when he got tired.
It seemed like a good life to me.
Papa Lee never got into the truck,
he would stand and talk to the peddler man.

The peddler man showed Papa Lee this big ole snake
he had just killed on our road.
It was long, he held his arm up high
its tail almost touched the ground.
I was peeking around the side of the truck.
For the first time ever I said,
"Geezalou!"
Mama Lee told me to leave the men folk alone.
I climbed up the red steps into the back of the big truck.

There were bins sort of like where the chickens lay their eggs.
These bins had beans and onions, and
nails and tools.

There was candy too.
I got to buy a candy bar with my nickel.
It was so big.
I ate that whole thing then had a stomach ache.

Mama Lee said she warned me.

I don't remember her warning me.
I wasn't paying attention to anything
but my candy bar though.
It tasted so good I just couldn't stop.

I was in some real pain
I just wanted to lay down.
I went out and laid down under the big tree
in front of the porch.

The grass in the shade felt so cool on my belly
and it smelled so good.

Next thing I knew I woke up
Hot breath steamed my face.
I open my eyes and the sun was so bright
I could barely make out the huge thing above me.
It was a cow's big nose attached to the head of a whole cow!

Her tongue was like a big snake
slowly making its way straight for me.
I jumped up and screamed as I climbed up the tree.
A bunch of the cows had wondered back home for the night,
they didn't even care when I yelled.

Mama Lee came running out the door
letting the screen door slam loud behind her.
She wiped her hands on her apron
put a hand above her eyes,
she couldn't see me with the glare.
"Ty Beth what is it?

She leaned out a little further to see if I was hurt or something.
"Mama Lee, come and get me"
I was crying, she looked at me again, "are you hurt, young'un?"
"No, I don't want to go past the cows, I'm scared"
She turned around shaking her head,
"Geezalou, them cows aren't going to hurt you, they eat grass"
"No Mama Lee come and get me!"
She was already back in the house.

I didn't know what to do.
The cows all got together and laid down right under the tree.
I was talking, to myself I guess,
"How am I going to get down?"
"I can't believe she would leave me"

"Maybe I can sing you cows to sleep"
"Twinkle twinkle little star, how I wonder what you are"
I remembered I saw a guy put a man to sleep,
on the Ed Sullivan show.
"You cows should just go to sleep,
you're feeling sleepy"
"I smell something good cooking,
I'm going to have to run for it!"

"Please God save me from these cows"
I jumped out as far as I could,
I jumped the last cow
just as she was lifting her head.
I made it to the porch.

My heart was pounding,
I had goose bumps all over.
I ran through the house
The screen door slammed behind me.
I was headed to the smell that filled the kitchen.

"Mama Lee, why didn't you come get me?"
I plopped down on the stool
where she was mixing corn bread.
"Cows won't hurt you"
she shook her head again
and pumped the handle on the sink pump.
Water came gushing out,
I got the dipper to catch me a cold drank of water.
Mama Lee, swatted my bottom and said,
"Go wash up out on the porch and use soap."

I used the bowl with the red line around the top,
there was a chip on the edge, the chip looked like an apple.

"Ty Beth hurry up and come in and set the table."
I loved her big forks and spoons and knives
the handles were so big you could barely get your fingers around
them.
We had little birds for supper.
Papa Lee said to be careful not to swallow the shot.
I spit out some BBs, not too many,
Mama Lee cleaned them really good.

After supper I helped Mama Lee with the dishes.
The smell of the Sweetheart dish soap was like perfume
the bubbles sparkled with rainbows.
Last thing before bed
Mama Lee rubbed alcohol on my chigger bites.
Then she would give me some of her Jergens lotion,
so I wouldn't be too dry.

I crawled into the big feather bed
she tucked me in
under her homemade down cover and
said, "remember your prayers."

It was the last time
I would ever
be there.

LIKE PRUNES, TWO ENOUGH THREE, TOO MANY

The last day at grandma's house was different.

We got up early,
Grandma has breakfast on the table.
Eggs and bacon with toast and store-bought jelly.
Grandma didn't like to make biscuits.
Toast was more modern
Store bought jelly was just as good.

I think she was wrong....
Grandpa didn't care if toast was modern.
He had biscuits.

We were told to bathe and put on our Sunday clothes.
I liked my Sunday clothes, especially my black shoes and lacey socks.
Grandma told me to come over the kitchen chair,
"Let's see your shoes" "hmm" she said,
she took a biscuit opened it up
rubbed it on my shoes.
They were very shiny after that.

I thought we were going somewhere special and exciting.
I couldn't even imagine where we would be going
in the middle of the week too.
Maybe there was a circus or something,
that was exciting.
We got in the car, and drove for a long time,
I was so sweaty.

Grandma and Grandpa didn't say a word
to each other the whole way.
I fell asleep, which I always do on a car ride.

When I woke up
my brothers were fussing with each other
Grandpa said he would pull the car over,

we all sat straight up and didn't move an inch.

I didn't recognize where we were.
I watched the fence posts fly by.
I hung my hand out the window,
the wind would catch it
and whip it up and down.
We finally pulled up
in front of this huge brick building
with white pillars in the front.
There were great lawns.

Across the road were rows of strawberries
farther then I could see.
The air was sweet and cool, I liked it.
My hair was stuck to my neck
with sweat from sleep'n in the car.
I'd be glad to get out and stretch.
We got out of the car one by one,

Grandma came around to make sure
we were "presentable".
She pulled at the collar of my dress
tucked in the boy's shirts.
Finally, we walked up the long stairs to the big doors.
Grandpa opened the door for Grandma
we followed her in.
The room was bigger than any place I'd ever been.
The walls had carved wood panels very fancy.

I tilted my head to see up at least three floors,

There was an echo with every step.
I looked up the stairs and at the walls.
It was cool in here.
I wondered how it would feel to lay on the floor,
but I didn't.

A big man walked across the big room
to greet Grandma and Grandpa.
He was speaking quietly to them and they to him.
We walked along a hallway to the man's office,
Grandma and Grandpa went into the office.

Us kids sat in big chairs
that felt like where a king would sit.
Randy sat with me because
he was too little to get in the chair by himself.

The hallway outside the office was long and polished
you could see the reflection of each window on the floor.
I couldn't figure out what this place was.

I was swinging my legs and my shoe fell off.
It echoed so loud in the big hallway
I was sure I was in trouble.
The big man walked out and smiled at us.

I don't know if I smiled back.
He talked to us as we walked.
I don't know one thing he said.

We followed him to see the cafeteria,
the chapel and out to a playground.

Grandma and Grandpa followed along behind us.
I kept looking back,
Grandpa was treading the brim of his hat
through his hands.
It made me feel uneasy.

We were told to go swing,
that's when it was becoming clear to me.

Why did I have such a sick feeling of total dread?

I watched my brothers on the swings,
laughing and being silly,
while I was once again,
screaming loud and hysterical on the inside.

I sat looking at the line of dirt in the grass where,
so many kids swung away the hours and the grass.
I showed no sign of any thought or fear,
but I knew

they were going to leave us here.

Why was this happening?
I looked up and realized grandpa wasn't there.
I stood up off the swing
my ears were pounding, where's grandpa?"
I looked around for the car
I saw my Grandpa taking my suitcase
out of the trunk of the car.

Grandma walked around in front of us.
My head was down when I saw her shoes –
black and shiny they looked brand-new,
I slowly raised my head and paused.
I saw her purse hanging on her arm,
her white gloves in her hand,
then her neck scarf.
I always liked the way she looked.

She took my chin in her hand and said,
"I think you will like it here."

"If there were only two of you
we could keep you,
but three is too many."

"You understand?"

You understand?
Who could understand, I'm not even 8 years old?
Like she decided she didn't want 3 pancakes,
so she threw them all away?

No, I don't understand!!

No words left my mouth
I just stood like a statue.
"You be good now."

she brushed away a fold
at the hem of her dress
and walked away.
Don't embarrass me."
She added and walked to the car.

Grandpa opened the door and she got in.
He turned around,
looked up the hill where we stood,
still and quiet.
He took his cigarette out of his mouth,
tossed it on the ground,
stepped on it.
He straightened the brim of his hat
placed it on his head,
walked around the car, he got in,
backed up and drove right by us.
Grandma didn't even look up.

Maybe we should have called her, Eva.

LEFT FOR NOW

The sign in the front of the building said,
Bachman's Christian Children's Home.
Was it Christian Children?
Or was it a Christian Home.
I don't know if I'm a Christian.
What was this going to mean?
If they find out, where will I go?
How did I miss that sign?

I decided right then and there,
I was not going to talk to or be nice anymore!
Someone took my brothers to the "Boys hall"
Randy wasn't even 3.
I felt like I needed to protect him
somehow,
I didn't know what to do.
I was to be taken to the "Girls hall".

We didn't even get to say good bye.
I told myself I would not smile,
or even talk to anyone.

We walked up stairs,
I looked over the railing
down to the big room
that had seemed so amazing.
I wish I didn't know what,
was up those stairs.

We stopped at a room.
One of the ladies said,
"This will be your room; do you like it?"
I cried.

She whispered to two girls that were in the hallway.
"Let's take her to the "Big Girl's hall" for tonight.
She told me to go with the girls, I did.

I sat and listened to the girls in the Big Girls hall, talking.
I was so lost and had no idea what to do.

There is no way to prepare for being,
left.

Nothing anywhere can prepare
a person to be abandoned.
No one could make sense of that.
Even the voice was quiet.
The smells were wrong
the noises were wrong

I tried to make sense of me.
I felt like I was out of place,
alone and lost.

Here in the biggest building
I've ever been in.
This place was filled with kids,
boys and girls,
big and little.
Were they lost and alone like us?
Had they been abandoned?
I tried to stay awake
for fear of
I didn't know what.

I didn't know what,
that was scariest of all.

The girls brought me some milk and a big cookie.
I listen to them talk about boys and school.
They were curling each other's hair.
One of the girls came and sat by me
and brushed my hair.

I'm pretty much falling asleep,
my last thought was,
how will Momma find us ever again?

Morning came I opened my eyes,
surprised that I had slept.
I was still in this place.

Getting up I pulled up my covers
like grandma had made us do.
I wanted to open my suitcase and
find my tooth brush and brush my teeth.

But where was it,
I didn't know.
I went to the top of the staircase
and listened.

It was quiet.
Fear almost made me not walk down the stairs.
I decided I might see my brothers
If I went down the stairs.
So, I did.

The first door I came to I pushed open.
Peering in just a little,
I realized it was the cafeteria and breakfast.
One of the big girls saw me,
"There you are finally awake,
let's get you a plate."

The food was really good.
The fresh strawberries were so good.
"How many pancakes do you want?"
 the girl asked me as she pulled the plate of pancakes over.
How many do I want?
"I want, 3"

I had some strawberries on top of my 3 pancakes.
People smiled, and talked so nice to me,
I could see in their eyes,
the way they held their mouths,
that they were sad that I was unhappy.

I just hate for others to be sad,
so, I broke down and was nice back.

The bad thing is when you like them
they can hurt you.
It was too late.
I followed the other girls to my hall after breakfast.

My suitcase was on the bed
in the little room,
my heart jumped,
I walked in and put my hand on it
for a feeling, it was just a suitcase
but it was a friend or something.

The Hall monitor lady
said to pick up my suitcase and follow her.
We went to a big room
where she opened my suitcase
put all my things into drawers marked
"socks sz 6, panties-small, slips,
dresses-small"

until,
all my things
were gone.

I wanted to stop her,
but I couldn't think of a nice way to stop her.

She was talking while she took all my things.

I never saw them again,
the socks and panties
that I got out of the drawers
were always stained and had holes,
the slips had the lace partly torn off.

Somebody else's panties.
Mine were clean and had no holes,
I wonder who got those.

I missed Mama Lee.
There was one good thing though.
He could not touch me anymore

TRYING TO... BE

I don't know how my brothers were
or where they were.
I was so worried about my little brother
he was so little.
I had a fear that bad things
would happen to my brothers.

When the weekend came,
we all went out to the strawberry fields.
There were stacks of big empty tin cans.

Each boy and girl took a can
and walked down a row.
I got one of the big cans and followed them.
I was looking around for my brothers,
but I didn't see them.

I started picking berries and filling my can.
One of the girls said we got a dime a can.
She said for every ten cans we could
keep a can full of berries if we wanted.

I ate as I picked,
she said that was ok too.

We had all sorts of things
with strawberries in the cafeteria.
I loved every one of them.

We had a big playground behind the buildings.
I would walk all around the fence looking beyond it.
I can't explain what I was feeling.
I wondered why other kids were here.
If they had parents and grandparents that thought,
they were too many.

I really tried to make myself

just let go of the feelings.
I wondered did they love me?
I was struck with the thought,
what is love?
Do I love them?

I tried to find feelings,
they were shut away.

I asked God many times to let me feel love.
Or no feelings at all.
I think I was broken.
I loved to pretend.
I even had stories that I thought were memories.

Movies were a relief for me.
I was able to see myself in other places with movies.
I liked movies with people who had emotions.
I found myself trying to learn them again.
It's difficult if you don't just feel them,
difficult to know which one goes with what.
I would laugh
when something was sad or if I was scared.
I don't think people noticed my difference,
I just stayed away from people.

That summer I earned enough to go to the movies.
We took the homes bus and went to town to the movie house.
The movie house was so beautiful.
There was red carpet everywhere.
The boys that lead us to our seats wore white gloves and a fancy
uniform.
The seats were padded and comfortable.
When the movie finally started it was loud
the music was scary,
it was very dark too.

The movie was very scary,
it was about a hand that crawled around
killing people.

I got a box of jujubes
even though they got stuck in my teeth.
I ate them on the way home.
I just squeezed the box at the movie,
I think I forgot about them.
Scared is an emotion.
That one I knew well.

LUNCH WITH A DOLLY.........

The next spring, we got to go to the Grand Ole' Opry.
I knew about it before from somewhere,
I couldn't remember where though.
We were the only people there.
We heard country music
heard Lester Flat and Earl Scruggs,

Grandpa Jones and a young girl they called "Dolly" Parton.
Grandpa Jones asked Dolly if "Dolly" was her given name?
She said, "I was born Dolly Rebecca Parton"
Grandpa Jones said, "Well I'll 'swan'
I have no idea what that meant.
It was funny though.

There were other people who sang and played in a band,
Porter Wagner and the Wagon Masters.

Their names were all on the paper they gave us when we came in.
I kept it for a long time.
When they got done singing one of the men prayed,
I think is was Grandpa Jones.

After that we went into a big room for lunch.
I remember thinking I would like to be a singer.

There was a long table with a white tablecloth on it.
There were nice glasses by each plate.
The best part was there was a brand new
one-dollar bill at each place.
We got to keep it.

Those people were so nice.
They wore clothes with tassels and jewels on them,
even on their cowboy hats.
I had never seen anything like it before.
I would never forget this amazing day.

LITTLE MEMORY OF THINGS

We drove into town on a school bus,
to go to school.
School was hard for me.
The school would sell the students a vitamin for .10 ever morning.
I always wanted one, but my money went to my account.

I had a friend in my class that got one every day.

One day she said I could have hers.
We got to go out to the drinking fountain
in the hall to take the vitamin.
I held it in my hand and looked at it,
it was brown,
small and round.
It smelled like vitamins.
I took it with water,
after I sucked off the sweetness on the outside.
I didn't feel any different.

I have snippets of memories,
I don't remember taking a bath or a showering
while we were at the home.
I don't remember any names from the home.

We had chapel twice a week,
I think it must have been Sunday and Wednesday.
I like the good memories.
I have always had a hard time with dates—
partly because I don't want to remember lots of things,
and partly because I just can't.

I do know we were in the orphanage for about 3 years.
My little brother was only about 3,

I know President Kennedy was assassinated in about 1963.
I think I can remember all of us kids together in the big TV room,
crying over the loss of a president

that we cared about
how did I know about this president?
My world didn't have presidents in it!

Another thing that gives me an anchor in time,
is that in the end,
Momma came to get us,
along with my Dad.

She had a baby with her,
my first little sister.
She was dark haired with green eyes
she was about six weeks old.
I know my sister was born in 1964,
because she is nine years younger than me.

I don't remember having Christmas
or a birthday during this time.
We ate meals,
went to school,
went to chapel,
picked strawberries once a year,
went to bed
every day.
Over and over,
days weeks and months went by
until 3 years had passed.

The day they came back for us,
Randy & I had just gotten back to the home
the night before,
we had stayed with a couple of ladies for the weekend.

One had fake legs.
I had to sleep with the lady with fake legs.
I laid there afraid to move.

I starred at her legs
leaned up against the wall
until I fell asleep
somehow.

Rudy wasn't doing good in school,
so they said he couldn't go with me and Randy.
It was good to see Randy,
it was almost like he wasn't sure who I was

I had bad grades in school to,
I guess Rudy's were really bad.

The ladies ask us if we would like to live with them.

"Like stay here all the time?"
I wondered what they wanted us for.
"What about Rudy?" Randy said.
They ladies said they really only wanted two of us.

We were driven back to the home.

The lady wanted to carry my suitcase,
"No please let me" I said as nicely as I could.
As we walked back inside, I went up one side of the stairs
Randy was almost 5 years old now,
he was taken by the hand by one of the older boys
and up the other side of the stairs.
I stood there to see if the boy was nice to him.
I watched until they went down the hall

I went to my room
put my suitcase under my bed.
The ladies had given me a comic book,
I pulled it out and looked at it.
I think if we hadn't said we wanted Rudy too,
they were going to adopt me and Randy,

we didn't even know, and they didn't ask me either.

This time 3 was a good thing.

UNEXPECTED CHANGE, AGAIN

We were up bright and early.
Breakfast was good,
we had cream of wheat
I crumbled my toast in it.
I remember I was very happy,
probably the breakfast.

We lined up to get on the school bus.
One of the monitors came thru the line
got me and Rudy.
"You two go ahead and get on the bus"
she pushed us forward.

We were confused but stepped up into the bus.
We both heard loud voices
looked at the same time.

Thru the windows we saw
something going on in the parking lot.
There was a car and a lady yelling
waving a paper around.

The big man,
Pastor Bachman was trying
to get her to calm down.

I looked at the lady and she saw me,
I was more confused.
She seemed familiar,
it was Momma!

I don't know how I felt.
I looked to the car and there he was,
looking right at me.
It had been nearly 3 years
the fear was still like it was yesterday.

The hall monitor lady told us
we might as well wait here.
Where's Randy?
Where's my suitcase?

We were finally told to go to our parents.

I wanted to run – but which way?

We were ushered into the back seat of the car
no kisses or hugs or how are you or
look how big you are, or I love you.

We got Randy,
but my suitcase was gone forever.

Momma looked different to me,
I wonder if I look different to her?
She smelled different to.

After we drove a few minutes,
I could no longer see the home behind us.
The bricks were gone,
the pillars were gone.
the strawberries were gone.

There was a noise that didn't make sense.
A baby started to fuss.
I looked around confused.
Momma picked up the blanket
on the seat next to her
She uncovered a dark-haired baby.
The three of us looked at each other,
no smile
I realized my mouth was hanging open still.

They talked angry
about how horrible those people at the home were,
for a long time.

They called them bad names.
I wanted to tell them the grownups
were very good and kind to me

I think the boys were probably alright too.

We didn't talk about being in there to each other, ever.
I wonder why now?

After we drove for hours,
we were hungry
Mom said there was light bread, mustard, and bologna
for sandwiches in the bag on the floor.

I missed the fresh bread at the home already.

We drove all day to my one of my mom's sister's house.
We all went into our aunt's house.
Us kids stayed huddled by the door.

Two little dogs were sniffing all around us.
Me and Randy were scared,
Rudy kicked at the dogs and they went away.

A tv was playing somewhere,
Rudy walked away from us.
We followed close behind him.
We sat on the edge of a couch.

It smelled stale and the ashtrays were full of ashes,
there was even a cup with cigarettes floating in it too.

I was so tired

I was trying not to cry.
Everything was missing.
A bed and a meal were missing.
Clean was missing.
Safety was missing.

This was worse I think then being abandoned.

A CHANGE, AND A NIGHTMARE

Mom called me in the kitchen.
She gave me the baby
told me to go change her
and put her down for a nap.

I stood there with this little baby in my arms,
"where do I take her?"
my mouth again, was hanging open
I wanted to say,
"I don't know how to take care of a baby"
I said, "Where do I get a diaper?"

"The suitcase is already in the room, they're in it"
My aunt pointed to the stairs,
"Go up the stairs
it's the first door you come to."
I walked up the stairs in a house
I've never been in before.
I opened the first door,

I stood there for a moment just looking.
I went in and laid the baby on the bed
while I looked for the diapers.
I started to change her,
the rubber pants came off first.

The diaper was very wet.
The smell of ammonia was strong,
I didn't know what to do with the diaper.
I laid it on a newspaper.
I changed her diaper as best I could
it was so baggy.
I don't know why my mom thought I could do this.
I put the rubber pants back on,
I hoped they would hold the diaper on.

I rocked her,

she cried some,
but she finally went to sleep,
it took a little while.
I sang quietly to her a made-up song.

I got tired, she was sweaty
I smoothed her hair back
and laid her on a blanket on the floor.
I put her little blanket over her
in case she got cold on the floor.

As soon as I laid her down,

he came in.

I got to my feet
backed away,
until I fell on the bed.

The whole family is down stairs,
the strange little baby is on the floor.
I thought I would die
why didn't I die?

I just left me there again,
Up I went to the safety of the ceiling,
that poor little girl.
She just doesn't have a chance.

Why God?

If you love little children, why?
Help her,
please help her.
No more feelings,
I just wanted to be blank.

We were packed into the car the next morning,
off again to a new life.
As thou nothing had ever happened.
Daylight came,
my nightmare started all over again.

I forgot until now that my Grandmother,
my mother's mother,
was there too.

Over the river & through the mountains

I think we drove for days.
We went over the Mississippi river
it was flooding over its banks and
over the bridge we drove across.
The Rocky Mountains were part of our trip too,
I thought they sounded so big and amazing.

My dad said the Indians were everywhere
they would scalp us if they could.
I thought of Papa, he would not like my dad.

I was hurting and had a hard time sitting still.
I needed to rub my pain,
I couldn't with all the people so close.
I made myself not cry
I felt like I couldn't breath
My chest hurt
But I did not cry.

When we finally got to California,
we ended up in a trailer house
on a Black Angus & Morgan horse ranch.

I didn't know anything about what this kind of ranch was,
but I do now.

There were two trailers,
the kids in one,
grown-ups in the other.

It was silly to me
I was so scared to be in a trailer with no parents.
I was terrified to be in a trailer with one parent.

I checked to make sure the door was locked
at least twice a night.
We had to walk through mud to both trailers.

We played a game getting to the kid's trailer.
We would jump from rock to rock
trying to stay out of the mud.
Nobody ever made it the whole way.

Something was wrong with the electric wires,
they hung down and touched the top of our trailer.
We would get shocked every time we touched the door handle.
I always tried to get my shirt sleeve over my hand to not get bit.
It didn't work to good.

It didn't feel like home.
I didn't know what home would ever be
how would it feel.
We moved sprinkler pipes,
got on horses,
mucked out stalls,
and lots of farm stuff.

Years later,
I saw a picture of myself sitting on a fence
by the horse corral,
I wore a cowboy hat and boots.

My brother told me our dad
had brought out a stallion to cover a mare.
He said it was very violent and we had to watch.
I don't remember it at all.

.

HORSES, HOUSE TRAILERS & ELECTRIC WIRES

I do remember smells in the barn
the tack shed
the feed shed,
I liked those smells,
for a while.

I remember night after night
trying to get away from him.

We were in the adult trailer.
Where was my mom?
How was he alone with me so much?
Retreating into the bathroom
was always what I did.

He would let me go to the bathroom
after I begged and begged.
I would lock the door and lay on the tile floor.
I would wake up in the floor
Then try to sneak back to the kids trailer.
I made it sometimes.

Our parents didn't get along at all.
We all felt uncomfortable around them
because they were mean to each other.
Then the physical fighting started.
The noise sounded like they were
going to turn the trailer over or something.

We could hear the grownups trailer booming,
the yelling and screaming, followed by quiet.
We all laid there awake,
staring into the dark
for a long time that night.

It turned out that my dad had knocked my mother
over a chair with a skillet,

or the other way around.
I'm not sure.

Grandma came again,
she talked so mean to us,
she told us we were making our mom sick
with all our fussing.
She pulled a switch off a tree and switched our legs,
while she barked,
"Get in that trailer, and get your stuff packed now!"
She had her tongue clamped between her teeth
like she was sticking it out at us.
I had no idea what fussing was making mom sick.

Grandma reached up grabbed our trailer door
She got a shock,
I was about to tell her not to touch the door,
it was too late– we all laughed.
We ran past her while she was dancing
around shaking her hand
swearing like crazy.
She was standing in the mud and not on a rock,
she got shocked extra good.

I don't know why grandma would come here
to get mad at us,
we didn't do this?
I don't know what we did
that made our mom sick.

Grandma said after she made our mom
come and get us from the orphanage,
we act like this.
She made her come and get us?
Why did she make her come and get us?
Why would grandma want them to have us,
she didn't seem to like us at all?

We moved away from my dad-- again

FINDING OUR WAY

My Mom's dad lived in a little town
close to where we had been living.
Grandma had to go home.
Mom's dad wasn't married to her anymore
I guess his new wife didn't like her either.

We went to stay with them for a very short time.
Grandpa Bryant was a really big man
he didn't hardly talk much.
His wife did though.
We moved again before a whole month went by.

My mom didn't have a job.
But we somehow were able to rent a small house
San Miguel, California only a block from the school.

We worried about nobody having a job.
I still don't know how she paid the rent.
I don't know how my mom took care of us.
She talked to the neighbors, over the fence
spent time with them.
I probably wouldn't have noticed but she said,
"I just don't know how I will ever take care of these kids"
the neighbor said you poor thing.

Were we going to be ok?

Mom said she was sick of walking across town in hades heat.
Me or Rudy would "get to go", on that walk with her
This big building gave out food to people
We waited in a long line in the sun,
maybe once or twice a month.
I hated to go, but we had no car,
we had to carry the stuff home.

We would get a big block of cheese, powdered milk,
powdered eggs, butter,

beans and rice, a big roll of bologna,
flour, sugar and lard too.
Powdered milk is not good no matter how you make it.

My mom could make the rest of it taste pretty good.

I had my own room,
it was an area off the kitchen
that had a sheet curtain across the opening.
I liked it.

My brothers slept in the little bedroom Mom said,
was off the back porch.
But, it was the back porch.
Mom had the big bedroom off the living room.

I think my sister Faith probably slept there too.
I don't remember if she slept with me yet or not.
We had good food and we laughed a lot.

Our house was always clean,
although it had linoleum that was paper-thin
with the design worn off.

Mom made me wax that floor till it shined,
even the thin parts.
Johnson's paste wax has
to be buffed for it to shine.

I drug my little brother around
on an old wool army blanket to buff it.
I would get to going real fast
make a sharp turn and he would tumble over.

He always laughed though,
his little fat belly would be red
from laying on that old wool army blanket,

but we had fun.
Rudy would make a running start
slide across the floor like he was skating.

Mom started to go to yard sales.
She sometimes got furniture
that was thrown away and recovered it.

She was really good at that stuff,
she refinished tables and things
she would sell the stuff she fixed up
for more than she paid for it.
She was happy.

She would come out on the porch
and play her harmonic or her accordion
while we played in the sprinklers.
It was nice.

He found us.

ALMOST GONE.....

He showed up at the gate one day
mom stormed out to the gate
she told him to get back in his car
and get out of here.

He said he wanted to see his children.
She told him no way and get out of here.
Mom had to get a divorce from our dad.
I guess she just figured he wouldn't find us again.

She had gone to court and was gone most of the day.
Grandma stayed home with us while
Mom had to go see the lawyer.
Mom got dressed nice and did her hair too.

Grandma would make us
sit on the couch with tweezers
and pluck the hair on her legs.
She had her legs covering Randy, me and Faith.
I think it was, so she could sleep,
and we wouldn't get into stuff.

Mom came home mad.
The little old lady across the street let her borrow her car.
She threw the keys to the car on the table.
She cried and smoked and told grandma the story.
Grandma smoked and cussed with momma.
We got sent outside but tried to hear what she said.

She lost, we had to go visit our dad--alone.

My brothers were so excited.
Oh no, how could this be happening?
Why can't someone stop him?
I begged, for a whole week,
"Please don't make me go."

Finally, the last day, I cried,
-out loud-
until I couldn't breathe.

I had nightmares that terrified me.

My mom said, "You have to go--the court said."
"Please," I pleaded,
"please."
I felt like I was going die.

I didn't sleep much that whole week.
He would be in my dreams.
Mom didn't seem to care
I was begging not to go.
She never asked my why?

She said she would send a tape recorder
with me in my purse.
What is she thinking?
What good would that do?

Why doesn't the baby have to go?
Maybe if I hold the baby?
My mom got an empty match box
put black tape on it
stuck the earplugs off the broken transistor
radio in the end.
"Here, put this in your purse"
she said this very close to my ear but not quiet.
I could smell her cigarette.
That smell was, Momma.

I put the match box in my purse.
But, did she think I was totally stupid?

My dad pulled up in front of the house,

we got into his car, and my brothers both said,
"She has a tape recorder in her purse!"
My dad didn't react at all.

I think I was mostly stunned
that they thought it was real.
We went out to Creston,
to a little bar /restaurant out in the country.

He told me to leave my purse in the car.
We walked across the dirt parking lot.
He held the screen door as we each walked under his arm.
He patted Rudy on top of the head
mussed up Randy's hair
He let the screen door slam behind me,
I jumped.
I don't know how I got through the day thus far.
I was resigned but desperately hopeful.
I was chanting please God, please God.

He put money on the pool table,
my brothers started to play.
They were squealing,
I was thinking maybe we would just
be playing pool and eat lunch.
I became anxious for my turn too.

Then he turned to me and said,
"Didn't you need to go to the bathroom?"
I didn't even answer.
He took my hand and tugged me toward the door.
The best I could muster was to try to drag my feet.

He stood me on the sink in the men's room
pulled down my pants and his.
I just don't know what happened after that,
I stood there just numb.

I was obviously damned.
No one could protect me.
I was just going to spend my life forever like this.

I was so sure someone would walk in and see this,
that my mind went black.
I was fainting,
I couldn't breathe.
I think my body died and my mind with it.
I don't want feelings.
I was falling.
I was almost gone

We went back inside
after what seemed like hours
my brothers were eating hamburgers.
I wanted one,

I got mine,
I ate it real fast.
I threw up on the floor
right there in the bar.

Maybe they won't let us come back here, I thought.
I think this is the first time
I ate my shame.

If there hadn't been 3?
Why had I been born?
Surely this wasn't a life worth living.
There would only be 2 and all would be good.

WEDDING, WAR & WATCHING BABIES

Mom said she never drank
or went to bars,
yet she met our step dad, Bill King
in the little bar in our town.

Those things confused me.
I don't think she would lie,
so I must not understand.

That said, here's what I remember.
He was at our house one day
when we got home from school.
Mom was sitting on the couch
with him and he had his arm around her.
He said hello to us
Mom told us to go do our homework.

We sat at the kitchen table smirking and giggling.
He stayed for another hour or so and he left.
We were asking Mom all kinds of questions
she was happy as she made us dinner
we were off to bed.

The next time we saw him
he was coming out of mom's room
early in the morning.

He started to come home to our house
every night.
We called him Bill.
Bill was tall--about 6'2".
He was a Sargent in the Army, a cook.
He had a big belly and a beard too.
He had tattoos and there was a black panther
the length of his forearm,
a naked lady on the other whole forearm.
Mom made him go get the naked lady panties.

He wouldn't cover up her breasts though.

He cussed a lot.
He would sit on the couch
in his boxer shorts and watch TV
He would have us bring him stuff-- mostly food.
He liked to watch anything on tv
that had country music.

He got a big "reel to reel" players/ recorder.
I ended up recording his music shows
when he was going to be playing poker
or had to work late.
I was supposed to stop the machine
when the commercials came on
and start in again when they were over.

He had piles of the tape boxes.
He loved them all.
He was just baffled when Charlie Pride started to become famous.
He decided that even though he was a black man.
He was a very good country singer.

My sister Andrea was born in 1965,
so I guess it was probably sometime that year
he moved into our house for good.
We had more food and didn't have to go get
the "commodities" anymore.

They were gone for most of a Saturday.
When they got home,
Bill brought in a 100lb bag of potatoes.
They told us that they had gotten married.
We were surprised but we didn't believe them.

He was going to be leaving for war again.
We had seen some war stuff on the news,

it didn't look like a good place.

I think Andrea was born when my step dad was in Viet Nam,
he came home when she was real tiny.
We moved to Templeton, to a house that was in bad shape.
The upstairs was bare wood walls and floors.

My mom just started fixing it up.
She did pretty good too.
We met our "next-door grandma" Lela.
She sewed and made quilts. I think she got mom into quilting.
Mom made so many beautiful quilts,
once she got done with the house.

Mom had gotten to go see our step dad in Hawaii.
In 1969, my sister Evonne was born.
We got boxes of stuff sent home from my step-dad
all kinds of things from Thailand, Viet Nam and places like that.
Some of the boxes came addressed to
Roberta King Templeton California.
The post office would call us or just bring the boxes over.

Mom put most of the stuff we got up in the closet.
She didn't know what to do with all.
Dad told her to unfold each piece of paper that was in the boxes
he was sending home money from playing poker.

Meanwhile we were in a different house in a different town.
With 3 little sisters so close together,
our house filled up fast.

I spent so much of my time watching the babies –
they were 9,10, and 14 years younger than me,
plus, Randy 5 years younger.
Mom cooked something good most days.

I was supposed to take care of baths,

help with laundry,
take care of them in the night if they were sick.
I slept with one or the other of the girls
throughout my childhood
I got peed on almost nightly for years.

Somewhere in all this time my stepdad came back
from wherever he had been
and lived at home after that.
We had to learn to have him around again
And not get on his nerves.

I ask him if we could call him Dad.
He said yes.
He was a little different when he came back kind of nervous.

He still got up to go to work early in the morning.
He would call me or Rudy downstairs,
to help him get ready for work.
He was still in the military.

We would blouse his boots
pinned his pins on his stiffly-starched shirt,
then go outside and start-up his car,
and get the heater going,
so he wouldn't have to get into a cold car.
I liked having a dad.
We didn't have to go with our dad anymore
when we got a stepdad.
The months and years of torture
ended.
I was trying to have feelings again,
I started with happy.

MEMORIES OF MOM.

My mom changed.
Mom started to be angry with me a lot.
She was yelling and hitting me,
she'd take my face in her angry hand,
then she'd talk in a low growl.
It made me very afraid.

Her breath smelled of stale cigarettes and coffee.
I got to a point
I didn't want to go in the same room with her
sometimes she terrified me when she walked behind me
a knife in her hand in the kitchen was the worst.

I can't pick out anything that made her seem this way.
I never could get things done the way she wanted.
I was a nervous wreck most of the time
It made me almost sick to my stomach.

Mind you--I know I'm somewhat lazy
I seem to forget a lot,
I have things going on in my head all the time.

I'd get caught daydreaming
when I didn't react to whatever
a smack to the head would bring me back.

I just wanted to get it right
make her happy
at least not make her mad.

We had to make food stretch for 6 kids.
Mom would cut the chicken
into more smaller pieces then there were.
Quarter the breasts and make
two pieces from the thighs.
She always cooked the organs as well.

One-night Randy said he wanted more.
Mom took him the heart,
that was all that was left.
He looked at it and made a face
"I'm not eating the wennie"
Mom turned around and tried not to laugh.
"Chickens don't have wennies"
she stepped back and pointed to the stairs
"Get yourself upstairs right now"
he got up and stomped up the stairs as loud as he could.

Rudy said, "I'll eat it"

Dad liked to fish
I never really wanted to go
I knew Mom was going to be angry when we got home
She didn't like being left with the little ones.

I liked it once we were there.
we would go out and catch a bunch of fish.
The hard part was coming home and cooking all the fish.
I would cook fish till everyone was full.
I could care less if I ate after that.

It was the same with pancakes.
Sometimes I wanted pancakes
If I didn't want 3
I didn't want any.

MOM NEEDS HELP.....

We had a short walk to school.

Most everybody had to walk by
our house on their way home.
We lived about 3 blocks from school.
My brothers and I would be
walking home from school.

You could hear her blocks away.
The curtains were open upstairs
where we all slept.

We looked at each other
not one of us said a word.
The mood had swung, as dad said.

When we got to the gate
she yelled from the window
"Get your asses in here now!"
I looked around to see who was in the street.
We were the only ones there.

My stomach felt like I would throw up
but we all ran
ran to our doom, again.

She was crying
she had a cigarette in her mouth
one in the ash tray
She had pulled everything out of our closet and our drawers
even the stuff my little sisters had under the bed.
Faith loved to draw and play school or store
she loved to keep all her "papers" as she called them.

Mom was screaming
how hard she worked to give us a nice home
this was the thanks she got.

We six slept in that room
we had a plywood wall
boys on one side girls on the other.

There was one small closet in the big room
one dresser on each side of the plywood

We were to get busy and clean it all up perfect
she would make us go outside to the switch tree
pick the perfect switch for our punishment
if perfection wasn't reached.

We heard that a lot and made frequent trips
to that switch tree.
I thought for a long time
that "Switch" was a real kind of tree.

This particular day,
my sisters were sitting, lined up against the wall
their knees pulled tightly up to their chests
arms wrapped tightly around them
little Evonne had tears flowing.
Faith looked at me and mouthed, "My papers."
Andrea had her chin jutted out, and a mad face on.

I looked over at them and smiled
behind my mother's back.
I just wanted to make them feel
that someone was there for them.

Then true-to-form for Andrea
she stood up and stomped her foot and said
"I'm telling MY daddy!"
Oooo, we knew we were in for it.

Mom stormed across the room
grabbed my sister by the hair

with her hands shaking
tears of anger in her eyes
"You're not telling anybody anything!
"Get in the corner"

Her voice was terrifying to the rest of us
yet Andrea wouldn't go.
You get in the corner and you stay there
till I tell you to come out.

Andrea wouldn't turn into the corner
we were all in shock.
Just do it Sissy.
I was wishing
praying
almost chanting it to myself.
She wouldn't budge.

HELP ARRIVED...

Somehow
our stepdad had come home
without us noticing
he was standing in the door of our room

He normally never came up stairs
it was surreal
His face was red, and he was shaking with anger.
"What the Hell is going on up here?
You can hear this all over the neighborhood!"

My mom threw the pile of papers
she had dragging out from under the bed
she was crying hysterically
"Look at this mess!

She had made this mess
I wanted to tell dad,
"she" made this mess.

They don't respect or appreciate anything."
Andrea and Evonne ran to their dad
Faith wasn't far behind
when she saw they would make it.

"You never help
these kids are too much!"
She stormed past them
grabbed her cigarettes
flew down the stairs, cussing the whole way.

Dad looked at us.
He ran his hand through his sweaty hair
"Damn its hot up here"
He paused for a moment
He looked like he felt sick
"Clean this mess up"

My sisters, one being carried
two others followed their dad downstairs.
We heard the front screen slam
We huddled by the window to see what was happening.

We stayed close to the edge of the window
tucked behind the curtain

Dad put the girls in the car
mom was on the other side of the car
She looked up and we were caught

"Get busy up there and stop gawking out the window"
I sat down on the bed
I looked around the room
trying to figure out where to start
I got it all put away somewhere

I kept a stack of Faith's papers and put them in a box.
I told her later that she could only keep what would fit in the box.

They came back with ice cream all over
I had to get them bathed and ready for bed.
Like nothing had happened at all.

There was no dinner that night.

This played out many times,

Dad didn't always get there to save us.

Dad was gone a lot playing cards.
My mom would get mad
why should I be stuck here watching the kids

She said she should get to go play poker to

They opened a poker room.
The Pine Street Parlor was in the next town over.
They ended up being gone through the night a lot.
We were to clean up
lock the door
go to bed alone on Friday
Saturday
Sunday nights.

I was supposed to take care of dinner
Baths
Laundry
lunches
homework and getting them to bed at 8.
The girls and of course my little brother
fought me all the way.

I yelled just like mom did.
I switched, just like mom did.
They all hated me.

Just like mom did.

I'm pretty sure my brother snuck out sometimes in the night.
I was far too afraid
to ever do something like that

You had to crawl out the window
onto the roof
jump to the apricot tree

I certainly was never going to do that!

One night I heard noise in the boy's room
like someone falling "in" the window.
He was playing, Inna- Godda- Davida
then I heard him throw up—

it sounded like into his guitar.
"Damn," he said.
I snickered.
He said, "Shut up."
I snickered again
I heard his guitar hit the floor
with that hollow twang they make.

BEING A PARENT

Sometimes when we got up in the morning,
they had left us a note to be quiet,
not to have the TV loud.

Sometimes they still weren't home
when we got up
or they left early again
I'm not sure.

I was supposed to feed everybody
and look after the little ones.

My one sister was very picky
about what she would eat
my dad made it clear to me
I was to prepare meat
potatoes and vegetables
--even for lunch.

I did
she would never eat it
when my dad would come home
she would climb up on his lap and
say, "I'm hungry."

He would jump up
pull his belt off
and start beating me.

I wasn't able to give an explanation
just try to stay standing
until he was done.

I decided that this wasn't going to happen anymore.
It was the weekend again
I cooked lunch, and as usual
she didn't eat it.

I sat down in the chair
across from her at the table
I looked her in the eyes

I said, "If, when dad gets home
you crawl into his lap and say one word
I held up one finger
I will grab you off his lap
I will beat *you* with this belt
I held up my belt.

She just sat there and glared at me.

When dad got home he sat down
she went over and sat on his lap and said,
"I'm..."
That was it.

She didn't get another word out
I had her by the arm
I swatted her three times with the belt
"Get upstairs".
She stood behind me in shock
"I Said MOVE", she ran.

Dad was so surprised he didn't move from his spot.
He just looked puzzled.
I was shaking and crying too
I was going to do this.
This time.

"I will not be held hostage by that brat anymore.
I cook for her
just like you told me to
she doesn't want it.
If you want to beat me—
this stops today."

I tossed my belt in his lap
went out the front door.
I sat on the front steps
because I dared not leave the yard
without permission.

I heard my mom, say to him
"Now can you see what brats you're raising?"
Was she defending me or including me or?

I sat on the step until it got dark
It starting to get cold
I walked around the house in my bare feet
in the back door and up to my room.
I was cried out
exhausted
somehow stronger,
finally, I went to sleep.

THIS RACE TO GO....

Whenever a new girl came to our school
I always made sure to try to help them
To be a friendly face.
Often, they would leave me
the popular kids were a draw

I didn't care I did it anyway.
That's when Bertha arrived.
Bertha was black.
Her hair was wild.

We became fast friends
we laughed so much.
We shared our happy's and sad's, she called it.
It was so good to have a friend all mine.

3 weeks went by and Bertha stopped coming to school
I never saw her again.
I went home and talked to Dad about it.
He said, "Did you say Bertha was her name?"
"Yes, she was my friend"
"They were run out of town"
he off handedly said
"What?"
"What do you mean "run out town?"
I didn't like how this sounded.
"Their kind aren't welcome around here"
He adjusted the pillow behind him
and got comfortable on the couch.

"Because she's black?"
would this really happen?
"Yes" he said.
"Go change the channel for me"
I changed the channel and walked upstairs.

Dad yelled behind me,

You won't have any friends
if you hang around with coloreds."

I could not believe people would do this.
I didn't get to tell her bye.

BOUND NO MORE...

The next year I started high school
they wanted all students to have a sex education class.

We had to bring home a note to be signed by our parents
I was intrigued to find out about sex education.
Mom said absolutely not!

Dad came to see what the discussion was.
I told him,
he signed the paper
He told mom I was absolutely going to the class.

She didn't argue with him.
She just said, "Fine"

I went to the class
sat way in the back.

I had worried all these years
I was going to have a baby
from what my dad did to me.
This hung over my head.

The teacher talked about body parts.
Then she talked about how
pregnancy is "achieved".

Then she said it.

You can get pregnant
for up to three days after having sex.
I did something that I had never done before.
I raised my hand.

She pointed to me. I said,
"If you have sex and 9 months and 3 days later
you haven't had a baby

you won't have a baby?"

She shook her head yes and she said
"Yes"

She called on someone else.

Nobody ever has to know this
I am not going to have a baby
I thought I would float off the chair
the boulder that I had carried was gone
My head was in a whirl

Maybe my life can change
What does this mean?

I was happier
I had been set free
to be a different "me."

I can be funny at school
even laugh at myself.

There was a boy in my Spanish class
he would always tease me.
He would say,
"Ty, why don't you come over here and sit on my lap"
I always had tried to ignore him
or tell him to shut up.

One I decided that I would shut him up.
I walked up and plopped down on his lap
"Ok are you happy now?"
The whole class started laughing and so did he.

I knew they were laughing with me,
that felt good.

He stopped after that.

I wanted to go to the homecoming dance
but I didn't have a date.
I was a freshman
I had an opportunity to serve punch and cookies
for the Juniors and Seniors.
I asked my mom and pleaded with my dad
he finally told my mom to let me go.
She said Ok!
Wow really?
This never happened.

I just hoped it wouldn't be like so many other times
when she would say yes
then she would make sure to find something
she thought I had done wrong
so I would not get to go
I asked her if she would make me a dress
with puffy short sleeves
she did!

We went shopping for the pattern and the fabric,
even a green ribbon for the waist.
She curled my hair
let me wear some makeup.

I looked at myself in the mirror and smiled,
but closed my mouth quickly noticing my braces

I walked out in my dress
twirled around
my mom looked me over
shook her head and said

"That's the best I could do
with what I had to work with."

I felt my shoulders droop
my heart too.
I walked out the door
the two blocks to the school

I was pretty
and turned ugly before I ever
got out of the house.

I listened to the music
watched kids dance
I pretended that I was one of them
That night several girls said they liked my dress
I would say, "My Mom made it" with pride
Why? I didn't want to have pride in it,
it made me mad.
Being at the party even though
I was serving punch and cookies
was still better than being at home.

I had to be home by 10
my dad drove down and picked me up
so I wouldn't have to walk home in the dark.
"Did you have a good time?"
"Ya."
"Did you dance?"
"No, I was there to serve the punch."
"Oh, I thought you got all prettied up to meet some boys."
"No!"
He laughed.

"You're telling me that no boys asked you to dance?"
"No, why would they?
I'm just a freshman."

We got home
I kissed my dad and hugged him

he hugged me back
I went upstairs to bed
I couldn't imagine that a boy
would ask me to dance
I laughed to myself.

APPEARANCES

We went to church most Sundays
when I say we
I mean my brothers and sisters and me.

We would sing, go to Sunday school
do crafts and get snacks
We heard stories about God and Jesus.
I remember going forward one Sunday
although I went forward a lot of Sundays.

But this particular one,
I was crying and praying.
I wanted to have a beautiful life
a life like the stories we heard
I asked God to help me be good
to let my mom, see that I was good.

I wanted her to not hate me
maybe even to love me.
I wanted to please not have to be so different.

I had gone forward to get saved
most Sundays *at the home*.

A lady there took me aside one night.
She said, "Ty, you only have to do this one-time"
"God saved you and forgave you,
He never needs to do it again."
How could it be that easy,
I was so awful.

My sisters told my mom I was crying in church.
"What? Why are you crying in church?
People are going to think you are abused or something."
I wasn't sure what she meant.
"No, I was just sad about something."

I was praying to myself, please God
just make her let this pass.

"If I hear of this happening again
I'll give you something to cry about!
 - do you hear me?"
"Yes." I said with my head down.
"God, I asked you to help me
why don't you help me?"
A week or so later
we saw a girl from school at the store
with her mom
Judy had glasses and long red hair.
She was smart and very quiet when she spoke
but she liked me
Her mom told my mom that she should let me come out
To ride horses with Judy.
Mom said that it was nice of her to ask
we would definitely do that.

I'm sure I was standing there with my mouth open.
Judy's mom said, "We can pick her up on Saturday
if that's alright."
My mom said, "Oh you don't have to do that.
I can bring her out.
My mother lives near your place
I can drop Ty off on my way."
"That will be fine, see you then Ty."

"Thank you." I said
and looked up at my mom.
She was smiling
she looked so pretty
then they walked away

It was like a spell broke or something.

"If you don't have your chores done by 9 o'clock
Saturday morning,
you won't go."

"Oh, I will Mom, I will."

Friday night I could barely sleep.
I was so excited,
I got up at 7 and worked like crazy
At 8:30, I asked if I was done.
There was no answer
I kept finding things to do.

Quarter to 9 came, my heart sank
it was going to happen again
My hopes were up high
enough that they would completely shatter
into a million pieces
when they were once again dashed.

Mom told everyone to get in the car
she headed out the door behind them.
I stood there and watched
she started to back out and stopped.

"Are you coming or what?"

I ran like the wind
I spent all day with Judy
riding horses.
We talked about God and being a Christian.
Riding horses was so amazing
I wonder did God send Judy?

It sure took a long time.

This big animal could just trot along with me on his back.

His breathing, occasional toots and the way he flipped his tail
after flies and bugs interested and entertained me too.

Judy and I palled around together off and on.
We were friends but not best friends.
I never really had a best friend.

I just never found that.

I had a few good friends at school
one was a particularly good friend.
I wanted him to ask me to our junior homecoming dance.
I was so excited,
but I was sure I wouldn't be allowed to go.

But, he drug his feet
another boy asked me
I didn't want to go with him.

I went home and told my mom that he asked me
but I didn't want to go with him.
My mom said, "he was the first to ask,
you'll go with him." then she asked,
"is it formal?
"uh..I think so."

Oh, my here's my out
she will never go along with that.
I still had a sinking feeling.

"Well we will have to look for you a dress"
"really?
I can go?
I had to go back to school
and tell him I would go with him.

This was a punishment date or something.

It didn't make sense to me.

My mom went to the thrift store.
She found two dresses that were both pretty
one a yellow chiffon and the other a green.

What has changed?
I got an up-do at the beauty shop
wore the yellow dress.
I was going to the dance.
When the boy came to pick me up
he came in
my mom took pictures of us
"have fun and be home by 11"

Wow 11 not 10, who was this lady?

We walked out to the car
we were going with his older brother and his date
He opened the door and I climbed into the seat,
I scooted across the back seat
he jumped in next to me.
The second he touched me
he got shocked by the static,
I grinned, and I thought,
"that will teach you not to touch me."

It wasn't awful, but it wasn't wonderful either.
The best thing was that I got to go on a date, without the nerves.
I didn't feel like I needed to impress him.
Hmmm?

Was I a meany?   Great "starter" date.

MY CONFIDANT.

One of the guys in our little group of four friends
started to give me a lot more attention.
It was so strange
We kind of worked into a relationship
kind of with ease.
Dennis was his name
he was blonde and tall and thin
with really curly hair.

He smokes
I don't smoke but I don't mind that he does.
He writes me love notes and gives me little gifts.
It feels so good.
It was like a drug almost
I couldn't get enough.

We kiss a lot and that's it
which I am so happy about.
We are so comfortable with each other
he even tells me what looks good on me
how to change my hair and stuff like that.
It's nice to have the positive attention.
I too am tall and very thin, 5'9" and 101 pounds.
My mom didn't trust Dennis
because he had a car and smoked.

I guess that's why, anyway.

He was so tan and handsome.
My mom would let us go with another couple,
to a movie and back home by 10.
Nobody wanted to be home by 10
just as well,
we never went to the movies.

I always wanted to go
but everybody wanted to go park

someplace and drink and kiss.

I would have loved to see a movie
especially when I was expected
to give my mom a report
on the whole thing!
I didn't really drink maybe one
but I didn't ever want
to be in a state that I can't take care of myself.

Dennis, knew, kind of what my home life
he was a good shoulder to cry on
or just complain to sometimes.

I had a birthday party for my 16th birthday
I will never forget.
I was told we were having a baby shower
for my 17-year-old cousin.
She was like 8 months pregnant.
They told her it was my birthday party

In fact, it was a combination birthday/baby shower.

I was the most disappointed
I think I had ever been.
I wish it was, anyway

My dad got me a "these boots are made for walking" album.
Nancy Sinatra was on the cover wearing white go-go boots.
I played it a few times just
so, he wouldn't know
I hated it.

They even invited some kids from school
I don't know what happened that caused, these events.
I can't believe it was my mom
my grandma probably told my mom to do it.

I never had birthday parties.
It was probably for my poor cousin though.
That's what my grandma always said
poor this one or that one.

Her sentiments were never followed by my name.

The end of June was prom
Dennis agreed to take my cousin with us.
I didn't want her there
but it was the only way I could go
because it wouldn't be nice to go without her.

She wore this bright orange and purple satin dress,
my mom made it.
She looked like someone smuggling beach balls.

I actually voiced my dislike of this situation.

No one heard me at all
the proof of course are the pictures
the three of us going to Jr prom.

Dennis was so nice
he felt compassion for her.
I remember when she finally
went to the hospital
she was screaming in pain
"I can't do this!"

"You should have thought about that nine months ago!'
Grandma said, "Get ready for some real pain,
it's worst then dying
in fact, you'll wish you were dead.

Just the birthing coach you want.

It was shortly after prom that Dennis and I split up
I had become attracted to a boy from Paso

I felt so different than with Dennis.
I wrote Dennis a note and he was crushed.
I couldn't face him to tell him.
But I told him in the note,
it would be worse if I really
didn't have 'those feelings" for him

(Years later I would find out Dennis was gay,
I would smack my forehead and say, Duh!
We are still friends today, we still squeal and hug each other,
he tells people I was his high school girl friend.)

WE FINALLY NOTICED

Things began to change again –
some bad some worse.

My mother started to have more of an issue
with my step dad than me or the rest of the kids.

It was still very stressful
their anger could be very loud and scary.
I think it started one night,
she told us to get to bed.
We all got up
said good night
started up the stairs.

My dad said, "you never hug these kids
or kiss them
or tell them you love them"

We all stopped on the stairs and looked up and down our ranks
in stark realization that dad was right.

I heard mom say, "they know, and I do to. anyway."

But, she didn't
ever.

We had never realized this.
It had never occurred to us to expect it.

There was sometimes a gift bought
for our mom by one of us.
A candy bar or something like that.

Because, she would hug you for it.
The little kids figured that out fast.
We were really a smart bunch.

Couched comments...

They went out shopping for a new couch.
Our old one had gotten all saggy.
Mom said it was because dad sat on it all the time.

Dad ate on the couch and the marble toped coffee table.
They both had gotten pretty messed up.
Mom was really mad that
her nice table was being trashed.

They were gone most of the day looking.
The new couch was delivered the next day
while we were at school.

When I walked in the house
I said, "oh is that the new couch?"
A sheet covered it
I figured was to keep it clean or something.
I rush over about to jump on it.
She screamed, "Don't touch it!"

I was barely able to stop myself
before I plopped down on it.
It was then that I realized it had little notes
pinned all over the sheet.

They didn't make sense to me.
All kinds of things with the words,
"that I didn't want" after each thing.

"What is it Mom?" I asked.

"Just one more time
when I didn't get what I wanted"
she was crying and real mad too,
He takes me to pick something
out and then says,

"that's not what you want,
we'll get this, piece of Shit!"

She started to whine
it turned into
a very scary almost banshee

I was frightened

Where are the girls? , I thought
I was in a panic.
I stepped back to peek in the kitchen.

There they were,
3 little sisters huddled together
at the bottom of the stairs.

They said all together,
"what's wrong with her?"
"I think she's sad, but it will be ok.

I looked back at mom,
she was writing more notes.
I stepped into the kitchen,
I waved the girls over to come with me.

Let's go out back and play in the yard
dad will be home soon.
I took them out back
we sat in the grass making clover chains.

They were having fun
I was listening for Dad to pull up.

"What the Hell is this about",
Dad was home.

They started screaming yelling loudly,
mom was hitting him
screaming terrible names at him.
Dad just kept holding her hands
trying to get her to calm down.

He kept saying her name over and over
which seem to make her madder.

He was mad,
you could tell by how red his face was.
He was trying to be calmer
than her at least.

Dad told mom she needed her shot.
I don't know what kind of shot it was
but she didn't want it,
she went into the bathroom
she slammed shut the door,
he made a call.

Is it over, was that it?

We all sat in the kitchen at the table
afraid to move or even breath.

In about 10 minutes an ambulance pulled up
these men got a stretcher
out of the back of the ambulance
they rolled the stretcher up to the front door.

The men had white clothes and white shoes.
They stood in the living room
talking quietly to dad.

Mom came out of the bathroom and saw them.
She looked confused for a moment,

then she was madder than ever.
They were telling her it would be alright now.

She flailed and cussed
as they attempted to wrapped up her arms.
They put belts around her
They gave her some sort of a shot.

Finally, she was quiet.
Mom was rolled out on the stretcher.
Dad walked out to the ambulance
and talked to one of the guys.

"What's wrong?"
I was following the stretcher out the door,
no one answered me,
I started praying, please let my mom be ok
please God,
please God.

Dad stood by the gate
until she was loaded up in the ambulance.
He said she would be ok
she just needed to go get some rest.

The next day when I was walking home
I saw a big truck from the furniture store in front of the house.
Some men carrying our new couch
came out and put the new couch
in the truck and took it away

Dad went out to the back porch
picked up the old couch,
all by himself
he carried it back into the living room.

He had a towel on top of the coffee table

He had a whole chicken
a loaf of bread
and a jar of mayonnaise.

Life got a new normal that day.

THE CALM, BEFORE

Dad had us cook and clean as usual.
The boys did dishes some
we got more treats like Ice Cream.
We watched TV a bit more to.

The little ones asked for money for school lunch,
so, we got to eat lunch in the cafeteria for 2 weeks.

I loved the cookies.

I loved everything they made in the school cafeteria
even tuna with cheese on a toasted hamburger bun.
The cafeteria ladies were nice.
I wanted to volunteer in the kitchen
one week a month.
I liked cleaning off tables and stacking trays.
Plus, when you volunteered
you got free lunch.

It was about two weeks before mom came home.
Daddy had gone and picked her up.
He opened her door and helped her out.
He got a couple bags out of the back seat
and followed her through the gate.

We were all so happy to see her we ran up to her.
She patted us on the head
and had gentle tears streaming down her cheeks.

It was very sad
it was unsettling to say the least.
She was not herself.
She was so quiet
after that she stayed in her bed for a while
then moved out to sleep on the couch.

We were told she was sick.

She stayed sick for a long time.

After a time, she started doing
some of the things she use to do.
She would be up sewing stuffed animals or
playing her organ at 2 or 3 in the morning.

Dad would go to the poker room by himself
mom would work on making quilts or sewing clothes.
She made donuts a lot then too.
She was so different.

We could ask her; can I go here
or have some of this or do whatever?
She would have no idea she had said, yes
she would be so angry with us
we didn't know what we were supposed to do.

As kids we still wanted to do things
she would shake her head yes.
So, we would do what we asked to do,
and worry about the consequences later.

Grandma Alice, mom's mom,
came to see us again.
She would always show up
when one of these type things happened.

She would be so stern with us always talking mean.
She was there to help mom she told us.
She yelled at Daddy and told him he should just leave.
He told her she was an old war.
It took us a few times before we understood
what he was really saying.

THE SMOKE NEVER CLEARS

Grandma had no hesitation
to pick up a switch and use it
for just about anything.

I came home from school so many times
the first thing I heard was,
"dump these ash trays"
"make some more sweet tea"

Grandma would say, "get me a paper
so I can write you a note",
she wanted more cigarettes.
Mama wanted some
my aunt wanted some too.

The note was always long.
Sometimes I would have to take an empty box along
so I'd get the right kind of extra-long or thin or something.
I'd head out the door with my list the empty box
the dollar and change for 3 paks.

There was always the "don't slam the screen door
and don't forget to get matches.

I
really,
liked to go,
anywhere – by myself
away from here.

It was quiet.
I came around the corner with the cigarettes,
the library bus was parked at the park.
I climbed up the carpeted steps and inside.

I looked around, new books everywhere.
I opened a few books

The protective cover crinkled.
Books smell good.

They let me check out a book.
I got one called,
"Valley of the Dolls"

I later found out,
It was not at all about dolls.
I carefully hid the book under my shirt.
I'm sure I would have had to take it back.

This was when I began to love to read.
I learned so many things
that helped me choose how I wanted to be.
Even table manners for fancy dining,
matching a handbag to shoes,
which sounded like
it would be important someday.

I read all kinds of books.
They ran like movies in my mind.

They were playing cards
still when I got back.
Playing cards at the kitchen table
sometimes went on for days.

One of my aunts, me or my older brother
would have to sit in
if they were short a person.

They smoked so much,
there would be an ashtray
either side of me
I would choke,
my eyes would burn,

my brother's too.

I was scared to play the wrong cards and
get yelled at or smacked on the head.

They would say,
"Stop acting like the smoke bothers you,
it's not that bad"
I probably have enough smoke in my lungs
to cause permanent damage
without ever smoking.
I just could not get how to play pinochle.
I hate cards too.

CHOICES HURT PEOPLE

I went to the park

I guess I snuck to the park one day at lunch time.
My friend at school wanted to go meet her boyfriend
she said he brought a friend.
I was stuck in that place where I didn't want to go
I couldn't say it out loud.
Dang!

Tony was there.

I had broken up with Dennis
because I thought I liked Tony.

He wanted to kiss me
and touch me.

I was trying stop him without saying words,
I laughed and moved away.
It wasn't working.

So, I kissed him.
It was uncomfortable and awful.
He was cute, but I didn't want to do this at all.

He called me several times
which just caused trouble in our house.
The yellow wall phone
was at the kitchen door
between the living room and kitchen.

I tried to get to the end
of the already stretched out cord,
so that my conversation wasn't limited to a no or a yes.
He would just be on the other end
doing homework and totally quiet.

I never have liked talking on the phone.
Someone was always there to make fun
or want to use the phone.
I was embarrassed most of the time.

I have a difficult time
talking to someone on the phone.
I can't keep focused.
I need to see their face.
 Tony was officially
my new boyfriend.
He drove a little sports car,
he was Italian
handsome too.

At some point I had gotten to the place
that he made me dizzy
when I thought of him.

I was 100-percent ruined
for the rest of my life in "Love."
After about 2 months,
he got permission from my mom
to take me to church.

Mom was sort of impressed
with Catholics or something.
She made me feel as though
this was a high honor
to have this chance,
at what
I didn't know.

NOT A PRAYER...

I was going to a Catholic church.
I was so excited to go.
He said we were stopping
by his house for a second on the way.
"Ok." I said.
I was wondering if I needed
to wear something on my head.
"Don't Catholic's wear something
on their head in church, or is it mass?"

I don't know
how it happened.

How did I end up in his room naked?
I was almost in that scary place
I went to when I was a little girl.

I was crying, and he said,
"Are you Ok?
Was this your first time?"
My head was spinning
I was going over it all.

I was mad, and in my head, I'm yelling,
"No, it's not my first time!
My dad stole my "first time."
I didn't want to do this,
*why can't I, **not** do this?"*

I can't talk to him,
I can just cry.

"Are you a virgin",
 he was really looking concerned.

"Well, not anymore," I said
I walked past him,

trying to act like I didn't care if he saw me naked.
If I was just really tough about this,
he wouldn't know I'm so destroyed.

He pulled me into the shower with him,
and I panicked for a moment,
because my hair got wet.
It took so long for my hair to dry
but then I laughed out loud
the thought of my hair being wet being a problem.

Tony took that as a sign that I was alright.
I was laughing,
I must be happy.

Because hysterical would not be
a normal response, right?

I was now worrying that I could be pregnant.
I had just gotten over the fear of this.

It had only been six months ago
I came home from school
with blood on my pants
scared I was dying.

My grandma was there,
and saw my pants,
she said she'd call my mom.

That made me really worried.
She didn't say anything else.
What was this all about?
I had no possible explanation.

My experience with blood
was only when he hurt me.

That was a long time ago now.

I went into the bathroom and sat on the toilet
I waited for all my blood to run out.
I had a bad stomachache too.

Some time went by—
I don't know how much—
before my mom opened the bathroom door
she tossed a box at me.
"Read the box." she said
and slammed the door.

The box said, "Kotex." Hmmm?
So, I read the box, the whole box,
every inch of the box.
I'm not dying!
But this is going to happen every month!
I was the last one in my class to get her period.
I was barely100 pounds,
which I was told in one of the triggers
for your body to start to change.

So, I was 16 years old,
and finally, I got the "curse".

NURSING A PIPE DREAM, TO POT PIES

My dad was starting to talk to me about college,
maybe my being a nurse or something.
I could live at home and go to a local school.
I would shake my head and say,
I'll think about it.
I was scared half to death
that I would say yes to my dad,
to be nice.

But who was he kidding.
If I was smart enough to go,
 if I wanted to go,
no way in the world
would I stay in this house one minute longer
than when I turned 18 years old!

How many times did I bring home
a report card with D's and F's.
How mom would yell at me
to get better grades.

I was probably the most confused by this
than anything else I could think of.
If you tell me I'm stupid and worthless
the best I could hope for was to be some poor man's wife,
why would you expect me to get good grades?

I got a job at the *Wagon Wheel Smorgie* in Paso,
I was making pretty good tips.
I actually started helping in the kitchen,
when I saw one of the cooks
tossing out chicken from the buffet.
"Hey, what are you doing?"

"It won't be any good tomorrow,
so, we just toss it."
"Why not make it into a chicken pot pie?"

I lifted my hands and formed a pie.

"Can you make a pot pie in a hotel pan?"
He held up this huge stainless-steel pan.
"Sure, I can I cook that much
most of the time anyway."
"If you can do that,
I'll put you to work on the line."

I went in the kitchen
put on a big apron,
he showed me where some things were,
and in no time,
I had made the crust for that big ol' pan
and started my filling.
Carrots, peas, celery, potatoes, mushrooms,
and chicken.

I poured some milk into my dough bowl
which had just the right amount of flour left in it,
along with salt and pepper
I mixed it with the vegetables to thicken the pie,
I was ready for the top.

I cut out some leaves from my top dough,
leaving vents and put the leaves around the top.
I brushed it with a slightly-beaten egg whites
put it into a 375-degree oven for about an hour.
When the dinner crowd came in,
the pot pie had filled the whole place
with that divine aroma.
The pan was scraped clean,
and of course,
I got to work more in the kitchen.

I made lots of comfort-type foods,
my meatloaf was also a big hit.

The kitchen people
thought I was super funny
we got along great.
I felt like a grown up.

I managed to save up $400,
toward a car.

One day, when I was looking out the window
of the restaurant,
I saw a lady across the street
pull a little car out of her garage.

She put a *For Sale* sign on it.
I figured it was way too much.
It was older, but real cute and real clean too.

When my mom came to pick me up from work,
I pointed out the car and she said,
"Let's take a look".
"Ok, why not."
I figured it was just an exercise in futility,
We looked at the car,
the lady came out and talked to us.

It's a Nash Rambler, push button.

Ok– that is old.

She wanted $250.00 for it.
"Wow! that's all!"
I could afford that!

Mom said, "Keep it down.
We don't want her to change her mind."
We got to take a drive around the block--mom drove.

When we got back, my mom looked at the lady.
"You been canning today?"
"Yes." She laughed.
"Put up a lug of peaches."

"Well, it is a nice little car."
mom walked around it, then said,
"I just need to talk to my husband,
but will you hold it for us until tomorrow?"
"Sure", she smiled big.
She was wiping her hands on her apron,
"I'll just park it in the garage for the night."

We told her good night,
mom added she hoped that all the jars sealed.
We got in the car and started toward home.
Mom looked at me and said,
"Here's what we do."

"Oh man. 'We' are going to do something."
I was grinning so hard, my face hurt,
but I couldn't stop.

TRICK OR SICK?

"Ok, we'll tell your dad that the paint is peeling. "
"But, Mom – the paint looks great."
"I know," she said.
"Just listen."

The smile was gone from my face,
my eyebrows were about
knitted together
by the time she laid out her plan.

She told my dad that
the headliner was ripped and hanging down,
that the paint was peeling,
that the tires were bald,
and lastly, that it smoked something fierce!

I was standing there
with my mouth hanging open,
trying for the life of me,
to figure out how exactly
this will help me get this car.

She got him to promise
that he would go and look at the car with me tomorrow.
He needed to take me to work
because she didn't think she could.

I walked in the kitchen,
stood there out of dad's sight,
shook my head.

She came in the kitchen
all smiles,
even dancing a bit.

She put her apron on and was at the sink washing her hands.
I walked over and stood by her,

looking at her and waiting.
"Don't you see?"
"Uh. No, I don't." I said
"Tomorrow, when he takes you to work,
he will be so relieved that the car is so nice,
he'll buy it on the spot."
"Now help me clean up some ball jars.
I feel like canning"

Well, she was right!
He bought it,
I paid him back,
but I think he would have
let me have it if we had told the truth.
It was the oddest thing.
I drove that little car home
that very night.

It was way cool!
I don't think the lies did anything?
Was it a trick or somehow sick?
I don't understand why
this was important to the process.

I had a car no matter the process.
I could only drive it to work and back,
but I was alright with that.

TOO OLD FOR MONSTERS

I had a crush on my photo class buddy,
along with every girl in school.
We were just friends.
Anyway, he was on his way to our neighbor's house
because they were some of his relatives,
he was going there to see them.

I was looking down the street as we walked,
I saw a man looking over the gate
at the neighbor's house.

Something felt strange.
I was almost going to vomit.
Why did he look so familiar?

"Who are you going to see today?"
"It's my aunt Gertrude and her husband Jim."
"What?
What is their last name?"
"Oh, Hawke."

No wonder I felt sick.
It was my real dad.
"I gotta go, talk to you tomorrow."

I had to walk right past their house to get home.

"Hi Ty," he said to me,
ever so casually.
I didn't turn around or falter a step,
the hair on the back of neck stood on end.

I was pretty much running
like I'd seen a terrible monster.
When I got in the house,
my stepdad was sitting on the couch.
"Dad, I'm so glad you're home!"

I sat down on what was left of the couch
in front of him.
His 300 ish pounds took up a lot of room.
"You're shaking,
you look like you've seen a ghost," he laughed.
"Its way worse than that,
I wish it was his ghost.
At least he wouldn't be alive anymore."
"Who?" Dad looked like
he was going to go kill someone.
I told him my real dad was across the street,
that he had talked to me when I went by.
I had talked to my stepdad
about what had happened to me—
at least a little bit of what happened.

"Ty, some people believe
there's nothing in the world
wrong with a relationship like that.
"They even say that they usually
pick the one that they love the most."

"Dad! That is disgusting.
Are you crazy?
That is just the worst thing I've ever heard.

16 years old, still not safe.

My dad looked up at me and said,
"Do you want me to go talk to him?"
"And say what?
What will you talk to him about?

No, I don't want you to talk to him."

Dad got up and went across the street.
I watched from the upstairs window.

He stood at the gate of the neighbor's house
He asked one of their kids to go get Jim.
Jim came out to the gate,
my dad reached across and shook his hand.
He shook his hand!
What?
Why would he touch him?

They stood and talked only a few moments,
my dad turned around
and walked back across the street.

I was downstairs waiting by the door
when he stepped inside.
"What did you say, what did he say?
"What happened?
Why did you shake his hand?"
Dad plopped down on the couch,
clicked on the TV
as he looked up at me and said,
"He seems like a real nice guy."
I don't think I was breathing,
I felt like it was a bad dream, nightmare!

"How can you say that?"
"Don't worry about him.
He won't bother you again, you're too old."

I turned around and walked upstairs.
I'm too old?
I am stunned.
I am scared to walk out of my own house.
I am so scared of that man.

I don't understand how my dad
could think the things he thinks.
I don't want to have

to worry about going outside.
I don't want him to talk to me.

I told the neighbors
that my Dad was a very bad man
and ask them to tell him
never talk to me again.
I would like to say
he never came back,
but he occasionally did.

PEEKS OF THE PAST

It was a beautiful day.
I felt really good.
Happy and light hearted.
I don't know if it was bio rhythms,
high tide or the phase of the moon.
It was a good day.

I stood just inside the screen door.
I was watching my mom
work in the flower garden.
I looked around the yard,
she had lots of roses all different colors.

She would always say that her
roses were as big as dinner plates.
I guess that is big for a rose.
I wondered if she had ever watched her mom
work in her flowers.
I decided to ask my mom
about when she was a kid.

I went out front where she was planting some flowers
in front of the house
sat down on the steps.
I watched her for a little bit.
She was very intent on her work.

Her hair was very dark and had beautiful waves,
she had a black bump on her forehead,
I remember her saying she had hit her head
her mom mixing ashes and sugar to get it to stop bleeding,
it left a scare.

She smiles with her mouth closed usually.
I don't know if it's because of how
yellow her teeth are from smoking
or the way her teeth are kind of crooked and chipped.

It's probably the yellow.
She always tried to brush with peroxide and baking soda,
and smoker's toothpaste sometimes to.

"Mom, what was it like when you were a kid?"
She sat back on her heels,
She looked at me with question in her eyes,
wrinkled up her fore head and laughed.
"What are you doing a report or something?"
It looks like she's in a good mood, I thought
"No, I just wanted to know
what it was like in the covered wagon days."
We both laughed.

She kept working as she swept us off
to a life of constant moving,
the efforts that her mom and dad
made daily to feed and take care of nine kids.

Mom had learned,
or taught herself to sew,
which of course,
ended up being a life-long love.

Her dad was very strict,
they weren't even allowed to
wear shorts for school PE class.
She said they would sneak shorts
with their mom's help.

She told me about singing on a radio show.
"Really, you sang on a radio show?"
"Don't act so surprised!

I had a beautiful voice
before they did my thyroid surgery
they nicked my vocal cords.

I still think I should have sued that doctor.
She got a little angry there.
I never had a "new" anything.
I got hand-me -downs that I
mended,
washed and ironed.

I found a sweater one day
that my sister had thrown on the trash heap,
I fixed the holes,
so, it looked brand new.

I washed it, and got the spots out too,
and dried it on a towel.
I got up the next morning,
I put it on for school,
my sister ripped it off me.

Mom seemed to be right back there,
pulling for dear life on that treasured sweater.

She looked far off.
I thought she was looking at something,
so, I looked too.

I remember us in a place
called Greeley Colorado
She looked over and said,
Never move to Greeley

Why Mom?

For one thing, it stinks there.
Nothing there but cattle and railroad.
My Momma was trying to keep 9 of us kids fed,
liv'n in dirt by the railroad tracks.

We had a fire where we would heat water in a pan
to wash ourselves with a bar of soap.

This woman had heard about a family
staying out there and brought us some corn,
I think it was feed corn

Momma didn't care she just needed to feed us something
The pot of water was boiling,
momma didn't want it to evaporate
before the corn cooked.
She grabbed the pie pan off the rocks
and put it on top of the pot

When she took off the pie pan to check the corn,
it had big bubbles –
Soap bubbles"
The pie pan had been sat down
on top of the bar of soap
it fell into the corn when she sat it on the pot.

What did you do?
We ate it
We tried to eat it
momma picked up the whole pot
threw it corn and all into the field.
When she turned around, she had tears,
but she was laughing,

She told Jerry to go get the pot.
We walked down the road looking for collard greens
We all walked along the road and we found asparagus
Just growing wild along the ditches

There had been 13 of us,
4 died, two before they were born
one right after she was born

the last one was about 2 when he died.

Where did you guys go after Greeley?
she thought for a minute.
I'm not sure.
We lived from Missouri to Morro Bay.

Somewhere in there they spilt up and
grandpa Bryant took the four youngest with him.
Mom, did you date?
"Pshhh!" she chuckled at that.

My dad would kill any boy
who looked at me or my sisters,
they all knew it too.

How did you end up with Jim?
I let him give me a ride home from town one day
My dad met him and said I could see him
We had gone for a drive
and fell asleep in the car,
when I got home,
my dad said we had to get married,
because I'd slept with Jim.

So, we did.
She looked dreamy or distant
I'm not sure which.
I don't know if she was kidding or not.
Not a very romantic story.

The phone rang,
she jumped up and ran for it.
It was a few minutes
before I got up and went back inside,
I was just savoring this most rare moment in time.

I sat there for a time,
thinking about the babies that died.
It was the saddest thing.
Being a mom who couldn't feed her kids
that would be most sad.

Later that same day,
I tried to talk to my dad
about his childhood.

He wouldn't tell me much—
just that they were poor.
He lived in shack of a house
that was so badly made,
there were huge spaces between
the boards on the walls and the outside.
So bad, they had newspaper applied to the walls
with flour paste
to keep out the draft.

That paste, in fact,
would be dinner sometimes—
flour and water soup.

His mom had told him
he was starving most of the time,
he had danced on the street corners for "ho-cakes."
I don't know what that means,
but it sounded sad.

Mom told me other things about Dad's life.
I guess that at some point,
his dad had a still in the woods,
they sold moonshine for what money they had.
That is, until this one day,
my dad was sitting on the porch
just doing nothing,

keeping an eye on his only brother
who he said was mentally ill.

A car pulled up, and two men got out.
They wanted to buy some "shine."
Dad figured he'd help out,
"Sure, come on, I'll git ya some."
So, they walked around the house,
he uncovered the mason jars,
"How many of'm do ya wont?"

I guess they took all those jars,
and his daddy too.
They were tax men, he called them
the revenuers.

He stood there and watched
them take his daddy away,
believing it was his fault.

They ate squirrel,
which had to be stewed for a long time
'cause it's so tough,

If I remember from when we
had gone to see our grandma in Georgia,
you needed a lot of gravy to choke it down.

My dad ended up joining the Army
when he was 16.
He lied about his age,
but they took him.

He had been cross-eyed since he was little.
The army told him they could fix it.
He did get his eyes fixed,
that made his life better.

He had been teased and bullied
for as long as he could remember.

Dad became a mess steward.
He was a real good cook,
cooked big batches of everything.
He stayed in the army
until he retired after 30 years.

I remember dad saying
my mom was the best cook ever.

I'm glad I decided
to talk to my parents that day.

I have more clarity about what produced
some of the things that made my parents
who they are.

I've always said, "The same water that hardens and egg,
softens a carrot.
If you add coffee beans you change the water."
It is of course talking about the same circumstance
for different people can produce different results.
The coffee beans change the water,
I think that means having a positive influence
introduced can change the outcome

IF I HAD TIME IN A BOTTLE

Despite everything else in my life,
graduation was upon us.
My friend Judy and I
were to sing *Time in a Bottle*
at baccalaureate.

I had a bad sore throat.
My mom was making my dress
and Judy's for this occasion.
My sisters were all over the place,
running and playing,
just under foot.

I herded them upstairs
told them to lay down for a nap.
They were complaining loudly,
but I told them stay put!

I needed some throat lozenges.
I decided I would just grab some change
out of my car and walk down to the store.
I wasn't allowed to take my car out
except to go to work and back.

The little store was half a block over,
and one block down,
one more block down Main Street.
I thought about the Sucrets in Mama Lee's closet, I smiled.

I got the lozenges,
I was slowly making my way back home,
just enjoying the sights and sounds
of the beautiful Mayday.

I saw a car zooming up to me.
It was my mom.
"Where the Hell do you think you're going?"

She was seething and had her lips pressed hard together,
as though trying to keep her words from escaping.

"I have a sore throat. I was-"
 She stopped me there with
"Get in this car."
 I walked around the car,
as soon as I stuck my head in the car,
she had me by my hair.
"I'm working on a dress for you,
you can't even watch those kids?"
"Mom, I was on my way."
Again, she stopped me—
this time with a hard slap.
"Where did you get money?"
I was now crying, and mad too.
"I got it out of my glove box,
it was only 35 cents."

It was only a half block home from there--thank God.
She ended up finishing my dress,
I was upstairs with the kids
until it was time for me to go.
I was so upset!
Here I was almost 18 years old,
I couldn't walk out of the yard
without permission.

I had no children,
yet I had the constant responsibility
for at least three of them.

I vowed, "I will never have any children—
and if I do, I will be the *mom*,
not make them do my job."
I had a hard time singing,
thank goodness Judy could carry us.

Everyone in our class clapped.
I actually stood up in front of people and sang.
Rather astonishing if you think about it.

FLEEING, THE VIPER'S NEST

There was a party for the seniors,
by some strange aligning of the planets,
the tides and her bio rhythms,
I got to go

I got permission to stay at my girlfriend
Robyn's house that night.
The next day was my birthday.
I would finally be 18.
Freedom was only hours away!
I felt as though I had been in a prison camp,
I could hear the allies coming over the hill.

I stayed at Robyn's house that night,
we talked with her mom
about me staying there
while I saved enough money
to get a place of my own.

We talked like we were both grownups.
I was asked what my plan was
how I was going to proceed.
I guess I had all the right answers because,
I called home the next day
told my dad that I had moved out.

I told him I would like to come over
later and get my things.
He said that would be fine.
I was really getting out!
It was like a dream—
kind of an unsteady
confusing dream.

Robyn drove me over in her car,
I was afraid that my mom
would try to take my car away.

Robyn's car had a radiator leak,
so everywhere we went
we had to constantly refill the reservoir.

We pulled up to my house,
Robyn popped the hood,
while I ran for the hose.
I turned on the hose
handed it over the fence to her.
She started to put it in the top of the radiator,
when the hose was
ripped through both our hands,
we both had cuts from the threads.
I was in shock.

What just happened?
Robyn and I stood looking at each other
for a brief moment,
I noticed Robyn's eyes were looking past me.
I turned around
my mom was holding the hose.

"You're not coming over here
stealing my water."
She was crazy-eyed
acting like we were thieves.

"Mom, it's just water."
"MY water," she spat the words at us."
I looked in the driveway
and realized dad's car wasn't there.

"I'm sorry Robyn.
Let's get my stuff."
"She's not stepping one foot on this property!"
I could see Robyn
really wanted a piece of my mom,

"Wait here, it will be Ok."

I walked past my mom
with fear of entering that house,
and not getting out again,
but I went forward.

My Grandmother was there,
she also was very angry.

"Why are you doing this to your Mother?"
"I'm not doing anything to my Mother."

I went up the stairs,
got boxes that I had already packed,
in hopes of getting them
out of the house before this,
I wouldn't have to come back.
My Grandmother followed me up the stairs,
she was slapping me in the back,
telling me how awful I was.
I just kept going,
I was not answering her.

When I got down the stairs with the first box,
my Mom grabbed it out of my hands.
"Let's see what you're stealing of mine."
I just stood there.
I was suddenly aware
I was standing tall and stern.
Was I getting some power?

I picked up each box
after she rifled through them,
handed them over the fence to Robyn,
who put them in her car.

My Grandmother had now
followed me up and down the stairs four times,
slapping me in the back
telling me how awful I was,
how I was leaving my mother
at the worst possible time.

"Your Mother is sick,
she can't take care
of these kids by herself."

After hearing those words
from my Grandma,
I finally snapped.
I spun around and faced her

"Listen here old woman,"
I was shaking,
"If you lay a hand on me
one more time,
I'll knock you down these stairs,
do you understand me?

"If I wait to leave
until my mother is not sick,
I will never
be able to leave,
these are HER children--not mine."
Moms take care of their own children!

Grandma didn't say another word.
She went downstairs
got a cigarette and stood by my Mom.
I walked past the couch
where my Mom sat--my last trip,
I was free.
"You'd better have everything,

cause you're not coming back."

There was no goodbye,
No, I love you,
just good riddance!
Maybe just, riddance.

This--from the woman who bore me.

I did not crawl out of her womb
some grotesque monster
that she was stuck with.

I was a sweet,
little curly-headed girl
with big blue eyes.

Every interaction said
she hated to have me there.

I was leaving,
why wasn't this
making her happy?

Robyn and I got in the car and drove off.
I was still shaking and started to cry.
I cried all the way to her –
make that "our" house.

Well, it wasn't anti-climactic.
I would never have thought
it would end like this.

Or did I?
I did have everything packed to go.
I knew I would have to plan an exit somehow.
I think I more than half thought,

my being 18 wouldn't matter.
She would hold me prisoner,
anyway.

I finally was going to be an adult
take care of myself.

When I am able to support myself
do all the adult things,
She might like me then,
maybe even be proud of me.

Maybe I will like her then.

I finally can be free.
I had an 18th birthday
a diploma
all my things
a car,
and a job.

It is going to be unbelievably amazing.

Why does my chest feel like an elephant is sitting on it?

PART 2

MY START...

I'm off to work as a grown up!
Wow, it feels so good
get in my car
go where I want,
I don't have to look over my shoulder,
or even fret over the slightest decision.

Of course, I fret over every decision.

I walked into work
a little breakfast spot,
I was actually whistling.

Why so happy? Mary asked me.
I moved out last night!
Oh, that is good news.
She ran and hugged me.
You'll be just fine.
You know that--right?

She stepped back
looked in my eyes
Concern on her face
sort of pride too--how odd.
Mary had encouraged me
just keep it together a few more months—
that was three months ago.

I made it!
I'm free as a bird.
a bird let out of a cage.
Not sure what to do.

I made lots of tips
headed home to my new digs
my radio turned up loud.
I was keeping time to the beat

on the dash,
the steering wheel, my knee too.

THE SLOWLY CLOSING DOOR...

What a great day!
When I walked into the house,
I didn't see anyone.
Anybody home, I said
In the kitchen, came the reply.

Robyn's mom looked worried.
"Are you alright – what's wrong?"
I was by her side—
puzzled that she looked at me so funny.

She was obviously pained to even say the words,
out they came anyway.

What did you steal from your mom?
"What?"
My head felt like it would explode.
"What are you talking about?"

I had both hands on my head –
it was spinning.
"Your mother called,
she wants the money
you stole from her."

She put her hand over her mouth.
"I have never stolen anything from her."
I was so shocked,
even my mom
would not do this,
would she?

"I'm calling that witch right now!"
I got the phone and dialed home.
I was so angry it was a good thing
I wasn't near her.

Dad picked up the phone,
I started with
"Where is she?"
"Who?" he asked.
"Mom! Where is she?"
"What's wrong?"

I told him she had called
told Robyn's mom
I had stolen money from her.

He was very calm.
"I'll get to the bottom of this.
Let me talk to Robyn's mom."
"My dad wants to talk to you please."
I handed her the phone
stood watching her face
as she listened to my dad.

"I see, oh I see, yes,
Ok, alright, thank you Bill."
She hung up the phone, looked at me, and said,
"Your dad assures me you didn't steal anything,
but he will talk to your mom
and call back."

He did call back about two hours later.
My mom had told him that she
made me clothes,
I took them with me,
they weren't mine.

She wanted the money for the fabric,
and to be paid for her time also.
He said not to worry about it—
she wouldn't bother me anymore.

"Why did she want to hurt me?"
She didn't like for me to be there,
but she wasn't happy I was gone.

How can I stop her from hurting me?
Why does she want to hurt me?

I got a small package in the mail that week.
My brother brought it to me.
When I opened it up
tears filled my eyes.
I cried like it was
the end of the world.

It was Mama Lee's bible.
She was gone.

I kept her with me
in my thoughts
always.

It was like a sad hug
from my Mama Lee,
just in time.
I held it to my heart and cried.

Papa Lee had died the year before
when his tractor turned over on him.

They were both gone

GRADUATION

244

That Friday was graduation.

My robe was pressed, my cap set just so.
The air was alive with excitement.
We had all made it through the gauntlet
that was high school.

Names were called,
people cheered as we processed
across the stage
receiving our diplomas,
it was still when my name was called.

No one came to celebrate this graduate today.
We all stood in line as people came by
congratulations,
cards,
gifts,
flowers,
and hugs.

I walked away with none of these.

I graduated

No one came.

My heart like a stone
my tears ready to broach
my attempt to keep them in control.
I had finally accomplished something,
nobody came,
nobody cared.

I will never be celebrated,

I will just go through this life from the outside.
I needed someone to tell me
I was worthy of anything at all.
I crawled through life as one taking up space.
I wanted to be loved by someone.

ON THE ROAD, AGAIN...

When I got home that night
I thought about the fact that
I was no longer in school.
I was 18 years old.
I had a place to live and a job.
All was not lost.
So far so good.

I parked my car and walked in the house.
Robyn's mom was waiting in the kitchen.
She said that she had thought it over
long and hard
then decided I would not
be able to stay there after all.

I felt like the floor fell out from under my feet.
What fear sprang up in me.
I have no help.
I have no plan.
Maybe all was lost after all.

I talked to my brother,
who talked to my aunt,
she said I could come stay with her
while I found a place,
a job, and all that.

I drove my car to her house,
It started making a knocking sound
then a banging sound
the car threw a rod.

There was not one tiny drop of
oil in the engine.
I had no idea I needed to check the oil,
which meant I was now on foot.
The car was toast in

Dos Palos, California.

I had no car again.

I cried angry hurt tears,
big tears and lots of them.
I clinched my fists,
but, I didn't hit anything.
I dug my nails into my palms.

JOB SEARCH GOES UP IN SMOKE..

God!
HELP ME
Do something.
This is too much
I can't take this much
I just want to not exist.

I applied everywhere
looked for apartments
--which I couldn't get anyway until I had a job.
I walked into town daily,
checking every sort of place.

I was really discouraged after about
three weeks
no prospects.
I spent the money I had
on a ten-speed bike.

I was feeling or more like knowing
I would never
be able to take care of myself,
after all.

I sat in the park,
just thinking of nothing.
Why would I ever think
I could take care of myself?

This guy walked up
offered me some pot.
Sure--why not?
It was very strong,
I was sorry immediately.

I sat there while those around me
we're talking about me,

I was in danger.
It was a long time until
I was able to get to my feet
I finally started toward home.

God
only knows
what could have happened—
that could have been
a terrible lesson learned.

By the time I walked
all the back to my aunts,
I figured I was about alright.
I probably smelled like pot.

They were making ice cream
which would not freeze,
we just drank it like a milkshake.

Milk always made me feel sick
along with the added alteration from earlier,
I was in the bathroom lying on the floor,
trying to throw up.

My aunt had called my parents
told them she was afraid
I was on drugs.

She had called while I was in town,
because they got there
about half an hour after I got sick.
Home was some five hours away.
I had not done a thing like drugs
before today.

I heard a rap on the door,
"Ty Beth, your mama is here".
It was my aunt.
"What?
What in the world is she talking about?"
I got up and opened the door,
There they stood-- mom and dad.

"Get your stuff.
You're coming home with us."
Why did I not even
Argue?

I didn't argue a bit.
I just got my stuff and got in the car.
My parents got in the car,
my mom turned around in the seat,
"I came to get you—
not because I love you,
or need you,

but because
you need me."

 I need her?

"I think my dad sadly said, "Roberta"
He must have made her
come and get me.

There was no other explanation.
The second time
someone made her come and get me.

There will not be a third.

I WILL ~~NEVER~~ COME BACK HERE...

I was quiet the whole way back to Templeton.
Why would you ever feel like you needed
to tear a person down
to being nothing.

It was like she had to make sure
I was completely aware
that in no way
was I loved,
not one bit.

I was of no possible worth
not needed or wanted.
What had I done to her.

I had resigned myself to the fact
that I was unable to take care of myself.

How many times had she told me
this best I could hope for
was to be some poor man's wife.

I had thought that the
magic number 18
would free me.

"What happened,
how did I end up here again?"

Robyn couldn't believe
I had come back home with them,
she came and picked me up.

"Why would you ever
in a million years go back there?"
Robyn looked at me like I was
mentally challenged at best.

"I didn't have a choice."

"You always have a choice,"
"Do I?"
I was now angry at me too

A DARK ROOM...

I just felt completely blank,
like my mind
and body
we're going about their own business
without my consent or input.

That weekend, we made plans
to go to San Luis Obispo,
a big college town some 30 minutes away.
I was determined not to let my parents
have any control over me.

Please God,
let me be strong.
I'm 18 years old.
It's like a magic number,
when do you feel like an actual grown up?

I decided that I needed
to be
someone else—

Someone who was tough and smart
and did what she wanted to do,
I'll be foreign too!

18 years old
this makes sense to me.
Robyn and I got ready at her house,
I told my dad I was staying at Robyn's,
he shouldn't wait up.

No reaction at all—just "Ok."
We got in the VW van,
and headed over the Cuesta Grade
to SLO town.

Robyn decided to go to this little bar
called *The Darkroom.*

It was full of college kids.
We sat down,
Robyn ordered us two beers,
which they brought—
no questions asked.

She said to just sip it.
No problem with that.
I don't really like beer,
I really didn't drink.

It wasn't long before
we had a couple of guys ask us to dance.
I talked to Robyn in some gibberish
that sounded German,
she told the guys that I was from Germany
didn't speak much English.

I was a very good actress.
Who knew?
This guy was asking me where I was from
in Germany,
I told him Cologne,
near Worms,
all with a very heavy accent.

We talked for a long time until
I got tired of it and said,
"Kidding!
I'm from Templeton."

He was floored.
"You have been putting us on this whole time?"
"Yipe!"

The problem was, that as soon
as I became *me* again,
it appeared that I was neither
strong
or smart.

Robyn wanted to get out of there
and go somewhere with these guys.
I tried to tell her I didn't want to go
she said she would leave me here
and come back later.

I wasn't going to sit in a bar
I didn't know what else to do.
I was a zombie.
It was like I was five years old again.

This guy was a know it all
To hear him talk.
He started coming on to me in living room floor
He was so self-absorbed,
he figured I must have had a good time.
Inside I was so disgusted and angry at myself.

My brain said not to let him know
he had power over me.
Act like you do this all the time-
-no big deal,
no big deal at all.

He asked if he could come see me
in Templeton.
"Sure."
I gave him my phone number,
even though I didn't want to.
I couldn't flat out lie.

Robyn later said, "Never give out your real number—
make something up."

"No need to worry about that.
This will never happen again."
I beat myself up for days
I felt I wasn't safe to go anywhere
because I had horrible judgement.

He called
of course,
ask me where I lived,
I told him,

I didn't have to leave the house
to screw myself up.
Turns out he rode a ten-speed bike
didn't even own a car.

He rode the bike over the grade
and showed up at my house.
His face was deep red, and he was
sweating like someone left a faucet on.

Mom wanted to know where I met him
The Darkroom, I said,
A dark room? she was appalled
Not a dark room, The Darkroom
I don't care which dark room, she spat

After he met my parents,
told them what capitalist pigs they were,

I moved in with him.

SHED & SHAMED

Six months later,
we got married.
When I called my mom,
told her we were going to get married,
the first thing out of her mouth was,
"Are you pregnant?"
"No mother,
I'm not pregnant."
"Well, time will tell, won't it"

She laughed like she was sure
she would be right on this one.
Mom said she would make a dress for me,
a shirt for him for the wedding.

"You know you can't wear white, right?"
She looked at me and did the
"click her tongue,
head shake combo."
"Yes" I know.
I was hoping for a pastel floral,
like in a Juliette style."

So, we browsed,
I found a nice fabric for the dress,
a complimentary one for the shirt.
We carried our selections to the counter
laid the simple wedding dress pattern down,
the lady said, "Oh, that will be a beautiful wedding dress."

My mom stepped up and said,
"Ya, girls now-a-days
don't want to wear white anymore."
How I continue to be surprised by her is beyond me.

Was she somehow protecting her reputation?

The dress was cute,
the shirt was too.
She even made me a little veil—
a nice touch.

We got married
In the little church that
we had attended as children,
complete with a "pound'n"—
which, if you're not familiar
with country tradition,
is when everyone
brings you a pound of something.

I had told mom that we needed towels,
ended up with eight sets
of various colors,
and a lot of flour and sugar.

The pastor had a small problem.
At first, he asked us if he should wear
his walking-around glasses
or his reading glasses?

My suggestion was
to wear the walking-around glasses
put the reading glasses in his pocket,
then switch them
when he got to the front.

He stood there a moment,
pondering, and smiled,
"That's a perfect solution."

He walked away with a spring in his step.
Obviously, he had thought of other times
when this combination would come in handy.

We had had to have
a counseling appointment
before we could get married.
The poor pastor hemmed
and hawed then said,
"Women are different from Men",
we both nodded.
"You will find she will start to cry
out of nowhere,
just comfort her until it passes"

Again, we nodded.
That was pretty much the direction
the rest of our brief conversation went.
We managed to keep from laughing
until we had closed the gate
in front of the little parsonage.

"Woman are different from men"
was said many times.
It was always comic relief.

This marriage,
of course,
was one of my biggest mistakes.

I believe
I was the only one I fooled.
But, of course,
my husband was too,
he fooled himself.

He felt that he was the most virile
desirable man on the earth—
at least he spouted that a lot.

I remember when he proposed.

He sat down to dinner
ate up everything in sight.
He was very appreciative
of my cooking,
for sure.

He scooted his seat back,
put his hands on his stomach,
"Well do you want to raise the GI bill?"
I was confused
that string of words made no sense at all to me.
"Excuse me?"

"If we get married,
they will increase my GI bill."
"Your check will increase?"
"Yes, so that's a yes, then?"

"Uh, Yes, I will marry you."
I said in my head,
I would love to increase your pay,
it felt like a purchase of a heifer or something.
To say I was disappointed
was the understatement of my life.

LEARNING TO PLEASE...

I really didn't want to be with him,
even though he was sooooo romantic.

I heard the words of my mother,
"You can only hope to be
some poor man's wife.

You have no other options."
I had better make the best of this
I decided.
I had been trying to be
everything he wanted.

I liked what he liked,
ate my eggs like he did,
kept the house spotless,
cooked big meals,
watched *Bridge Over the River Kwai*,
over and over.

He had to take me all over,
to put in applications for work.
I didn't even want to try.

I went into some of the places
waited a minute
went back to the car
told him they weren't hiring,

I think now,
I was in a big way passive-aggressive.
He was extremely boisterous,
his opinions were gospel.

Seriously, anyone who disagreed with him
was an obvious idiot.
He had a "get-good-grades" brain,

but not so much,
"come-out-of-the-rain" brain.

I, on the other hand,
had lots of day-to-day common sense,
but couldn't make my voice heard.

He had pushed me to start
some classes at the city college,
although I was sure it was a waste of time.

I just wasn't smart enough for college.
Why would he make me do this
it would be a waste of time and money.

He got me a job
at the college cleaning classrooms.
He was very proud of himself.
He would go pick up my check too.

I stopped wanting to please him.
I didn't want to do anything he wanted me to.

ELEPHANTS & MEMORIES

One day, I was waiting for my class to start,
just sitting on a picnic table
outside the Psychology classroom.

The class was watching
a video about elephants.
I decided to peek in,
I saw a little baby, pinkish gray elephant
standing almost underneath his big mother,
swaying back and forth slowly.

The professor pointed to the chain
around the leg of the baby elephant,
then to the chain around the leg
of the enormous mother elephant.

The two chains were the same.
I got closer,
so I could hear what he was saying.

"The chains are put on the elephant as a baby,
the baby learns that he cannot escape that chain
and stops trying.

That same chain is used for his whole life.
He won't even try to break it,
because, he's broken."

I stood there puzzled.
"That is what happens to people
who experience abuse,
physical or mental—
both equally effective.

They become sure that they
are unable to do anything about it,
and are resigned to continue,

not only their lives that way,
but also, to pass it from generation
to generation.

It is quite difficult for these
people to change their lives,
they are completely
chained to the idea
that their situation
is set in stone forever.

Am I a baby elephant?
I have to break the chain,
somehow.

I walked around campus for a while,
just thinking.
I came around this corner,
there were a couple of girls
sitting on the stairs
next to a building.
They caught my eye
stopped me in my tracks.
I flashed back in time to the orphanage.

I had taken a rolling basket of clothes
over to the laundry area.
I walked inside and could smell
the hot soapy water.

I saw huge barrels of powdered detergent;
the smell burned my nose.
There were giant commercial washers and dryers,
and concrete floors.
The smell of soap and damp concrete
was heavy in the air.

I parked the cart inside,
turned to leave,
two girls were in the doorway.
My stomach gnarled,
it took my breath away.
I was immediately on alert.

"Hey, what are you doing over on
the big-girls' side?"
They walked over to me,
one girl put her hand on my shoulder
the other went around behind me
urging me forward.

"I'm supposed to get straight back."
The girls were now on either side of me,
herding me toward the wooden stairs
on the side of the building.
"Come sit and talk to us for a few minutes."

I felt sick, but I couldn't say anything.
The girls sat down next to me,
pulled up their skirts, they weren't wearing panties.
"let's play for a little while
and you can go back to
the little-girl's side.
I was once again held prisoner
they weren't holding me
I was.

"Why? God, why?
Help me--please someone help me!"
I decided to run,

I jumped up and ran as fast as I could.
I could smell them.
I gagged and threw up.

I told the hall matron that the soap made me feel sick,
they didn't make me go to the laundry room anymore.

I don't know why
I got that memory right then,
but I would have many such incidents
where a smell or a sight
would transport me to another place.

What a long day that was.

Even looking back,
I was emotionally wiped out,
as though this experience
had occurred today.

I got an A in my American history class
I got a B+ in my Lit class.
We were supposed to give our opinion on
Kafka's or Solzhenitsyn's Bug story.
The Metamorphosis
I could use one of those myself

The professor marked me down
for my "opinion" ?
Never will understand that one.
Once again
Confirmation,
my opinion doesn't matter
and it's wrong.

I was failing Geology, so I dropped the class.

The last class was Art History,
we painted to.
We were having a nude model,
I told Mike about it

Mistake.

The teacher wanted us
to exaggerate the features of our model.
She sauntered over to the couch and slowly dropped
her flannel Indian print men's robe.

Our model was about 250 pounds of
Rodan-esk woman.

Mike made sure he came "early" to meet me.
He was grossly disgusted and mad.
His words.

RIGHT OR NOT, HERE I AM...

Surprising as it was, at some point the sweetness
(imitation on my side)
Between my husband and I
turned sour,
wore off
died.

I can't put my finger on what went wrong,
although it was very likely the sweatiness
or when I had an opinion
that I felt strongly about –
one that differed from my husband's.

He quite literally believed,
and still does today,
that *his* is the only opinion that is correct,
or that matters.

This was amazing, because of all the people
I tried to assert myself with,
he was the all-time worst.

I truly believed that if I said
something was black,
he said it was white,
not only white,
but any idiot would clearly
see it was white.
I wasn't even up to "idiot".

I tried to be what he wanted in every way,
as much as it was possible for me.
I can remember telling him about something
from my childhood, and he would say,
"You think that was bad—
well this is what happened to me!"
I told him I didn't want to have an

"I had it worse than you did contest."

Granted, he lived with a stepfather
who was a mean drunk,
according to him,
who had no problem with beating him.

He told stories of wearing
black socks to school,
which his father objected to,
a sign of being wild at that time.

He would put those black socks every morning.
He would walk down the stairs
knowing full well
he was going to get beaten,
but he'd do it anyway.

His father finally gave in
told him he could wear the black socks
to two days a week.

He chose Saturday and Sunday,
because he thought he should be able to
wear them any day he wanted.

I told him his dad had a problem alright.
He, of course, thought I was referring to the beating.
I was thinking more of the strong-willed idiot.
I think he was "up to" idiot.

SMOKE AND CINDERS

I started to meet other college-aged people
I was beginning to have my world expanded
thoughts and feelings and actions too.
I drank beer on occasion and wine sometimes too.
Pot was everywhere.
I didn't care for it.
I couldn't believe how people just lit up
anywhere they were—
breakfast time, driving-to-school time,
lunch time, driving home,
before dinner,
after dinner.

I just couldn't understand how people coped
with life and living,
when they were—
well--altered all the time.

For me, it just came down to safety.
I could not take care of myself if I was altered –
whether it was drugs or alcohol.
This is not to say I have never been altered,
because I have thrown up my toenails
from too much drinking
and getting carried away having fun.

But, I do believe I have learned my lesson.
Funny, how often that statement is preceded by,
or followed by, a sad revelation.

I started to see that
I could make choices,
but sometimes *seeing* and *doing*
were far apart.

It was one of the first times
I was able to say "no" to things—

well, at least some things that I didn't want.

Frequently, I made a choice not to choose.
My will and my rights weren't important.
The happiness of everybody else
was supremely more important to me.
At least that's what I thought.

I now believe that I needed,
with every fiber in my body,
to please everybody,
whereby proving that I was
completely loveable
and worthy.

I was dragged into many dark
terrible places by my husband,
following his lust.
He needed for me to do whatever he wanted to do.
I am still haunted by the things he made me do.
The control he had over me was dark
and came from fear.

He is still the father of my children,
he was, and they are important to me.

My children, because they are amazing gifts,
their father, because,
and only because,
they love him.
.

I will always treat him with respect,
I would any other human,
never make them feel that they can't see, talk to,
or spend time with him,
and have nothing but joy from me about it.
Even with all the dark and sadness,

I did learn to be self-sacrificing,
I do dearly love, and work for the happiness
of my family and friends—
which is wonderfully reciprocated.

My three sons,
which are wonderful,
my complete joy.

I wish that I could say that we worked everything out,
lived happily ever after,
but not so much.

SHREDDED REFLECTION OF LIFE

I was more and more miserable,
I was grotesquely ugly,
No redeeming quality at all.

After being told one evening that I was
stupid,
fat,
and ugly

I quickly replied,
"I am not fat!"

Whoa- what's wrong with this picture?
My answer was out of my mouth
Before I knew I said it.

Weight was the only thing
I thought I could control.

He told me daily,
whether by words,
actions,
or just a look,
that I was unappealing and a burden.

If I had a nickel for every time he said,
"If it weren't for you and these kids,
I could have a decent life."

I was too pale
and too flat-chested—
at least they were the main complaints.

He was,
at one point,
going to bring home an inmate
along with his girlfriend,

from where he worked –
as soon as the guy got released –
to show us some sex tricks,

He was actively discussing with some inmate
his problems with his wife
he was planning to get some help.
My sex life with my husband was disgusting,
to say the least.
I was not involved,
it didn't matter,
because I would have just been
more frustrated.

He told me I was frigid.
To my utter chagrined
I tried to get better.

I watched "Coal Miner's Daughter", one night
there was a scene that was supposed to be
their wedding night.

It perfectly reenacted what mine was.
Sweat dripping all over
he didn't even know I was there.
He never even noticed
the horrified look of disgust on my face.

I watched a talk show one day
that talked about sexual relationships in marriage.
They said you needed to talk to each other,
say what you want,
that maybe he just doesn't know.
Hmmmm? Ok.

It took so much will to finally say to him,
"When we *do-it*,

could you touch my breasts?"
I was barely able to keep myself from putting
my hands over my mouth
as the words took flight.

He jumped up with such disgust,
"What are you gay or something?"
I just looked at him.
My mouth now hanging open,
even I knew he was ignorant.

That night, he had sex,
he was sweating,
dripping sweat in my face,
I was just trying to keep it
out of my eyes and mouth.
He was done,

I started to get up and go clean up
"Why do you do that?" He was mad.
"Most women just enjoy lying there,
even going to sleep like that."

I had to try to sleep like that all night,
I dared not try to get up.
How the heck did he
know what "most women" enjoyed?

DEHUMANIZATION COMPLETE

I didn't want to clean the house
do dishes or laundry either.
I was headed into depression.

When he came in the door after work
one night he had a bag in his hand.
"Here go try this on"
"What is it?" I was peering into the bag.

"Just put it on and come show me."
It was a one-piece bathing suit.
Brown
I hated the way I looked in it.
I walked out to show him

"Hmmm, turn around"
I turned around.
He came up and cupped my small breast.
"The lady at the store said
this would make you
look like you had boobs"

"The criss-cross in the front or something?
I guess it's better,
a little"

He had gone to a store
talked to someone
about his very flat chested wife
that person had helped him
or me out?

I wonder if the sales person
saw him for the ignorant jerk he is.
I was so angry and hurt.

How could he ever hurt me more?

He did over and over

I could never get to a place
where he didn't hurt me.
I ask him why he was so abusive?
He said, "I've never hit you"
I said, "There are other ways to abuse a person."

He stood up and ran
both hands through his curly hair,
then told me,
"mental abuse was not a real thing."
"TV idiots came up with mental abuse
to make men look like the problem."

How do you answer something that stupid?

It was that night,
after hearing
how unattractive I was
for the last time,

I went to work so upset
I could hardly think.
This job was his command.
I needed to contribute something.
Nights work was most convenient
for him.

A guy came in, a regular.
He said he hated to see me so upset,
that I should just go for a ride with him
after work.
I said no way.
He continued to sweet talk me,
just a drive.
"No"

I got a call from my husband
He was angry and loud,
wanting to know when I got off
he was tired of watching the kids.

He started yelling at me for something.
I told him I had to go.
He decided that I was still
"pissing & moaning"
I had better knock it off.
I hung up.

Long story short—
I went for the ride.
I thought, of course,
we were just going for a ride.

I was such an idiot.
Even I, am sick of me
being such an idiot.

Of course, there was sex.
I didn't want to,
I felt like I was going
to get in some big trouble
at home anyway,
maybe this would get me out
of the whole situation.

Wow, that was what sex was supposed to be like!
I was in shock.
I'm supposed to like it, and I did!
He was interested in me and my body,
he made me feel so sexy and beautiful.

I UNRAVELED...MY WORLD

We drove back to my car.
Romance over,
I got out and he sped off.

The two cop cars by my car
may have had something to do with that.
They looked at me
like I was disgusting.

They said, "You better get yourself home
your husband is worried."

I was mad he'd called the police.
The cops were total jerks.
I had to go home to face the music.
I didn't know what he would do.
I was going to be tough.

By the time I got home,
I had lost the bravery
I was going to have.
He met me at the front gate
with a gun.

He had a handful of my hair,
slung me through the gate
onto the driveway,
I was in survival mode.

My hands and knees were cut and bleeding,
but I didn't even realize it until later.
I scrambled to get away.

'Where have you been?"
He grabbed me up again
sent me tumbling toward the lawn.
"Nowhere."

I was in total self-preservation.
"Nowhere, I swear."
"You lying bitch!" He was fuming.
"I can smell sex on you!"
"NO – NO, I didn't."

I was in fear of my life,
I felt like I deserved
whatever happened.
What was wrong with me!

He started tearing at my clothes,
I was naked in our front yard,
he raped me.
It was my husband,
and it was rape.

"I can tell you were with someone else."
He was so excited,
it was the most horrifying thing
I've ever experienced,
at least to that point in time.

He smacked me in the head
with the gun and said,
"Get in the house."

I was grabbing my clothes
running for the door.
He came in right behind me,
grabbed my hair again,
just kept going to the bedroom.

"Get on the bed."
He was shutting the door
pulled off his shirt.
I sat on the side of the bed,

which pissed him off again.

"GET ON THE BED!"
He was waving the gun around
jumped on top of me.

I could barely breathe
he sat on my chest with
his knees on my forearms.

Why hadn't I learned
how to get out of this situation.
I know I'd seen it on TV.

One hand was on my mouth,
the other had the gun on my forehead.

I was wildly thrashing,
I could not move him.
He hit me in the side of the head
with the gun
again,
which was so painful I almost passed out.

"So, by rights,
I should just kill you,
I really like this bed,
it will be ruined."
I was sure I was going to die,
it was my fault.

My babies…

"If I shoot you here,"
he stuck the gun in my mouth,
"I will be stuck with those kids."
He had one hand on my throat,

I was gasping for air.

I was starting to pass out,
I heard a tinkling, then blackness.
Next thing I knew, he was shaking me,
"Don't you die yet bitch."

"I'm not dead."
I opened my eyes,
he looked relieved.
"Just go to sleep,
we'll talk about this tomorrow."

He took off his pants,
turned off the lamp,
and got in bed.
I couldn't move—
I was totally paralyzed with fear.

Suddenly he was mad again.
"Stop acting like you're afraid of me!"

I didn't move.
He pulled back both feet
kicked me out of the bed into the wall.
I was scrambling for the door,
knowing I only had one chance.

I managed to get the door open
get to the living room,
as he caught me again by the hair,
slammed me into the rocking chair.

He grabbed my throat again
with both hands and was pressing
so hard I thought
he would break my neck.

My little sister and the baby
we're sleeping in the room
behind that wall.
I hoped they were asleep anyway.

Then suddenly, for some reason,
he stopped and stood up,
very calmly he said,
"Let's go back to bed,
we'll talk about this tomorrow."

I was shocked
when the morning came,
I was alive,
he was gone to work
at the prison.

I called the police,
they took me
and my kids to a women's shelter.

The place smelled bad,
like dirty diapers
and stale cigarettes.

It was awful,
after one night
I wanted out.

The noise was constant.
There was a lot of crying
Both women and children
I told them I wanted to go home,
make him leave.
We were renting
from some friends,

They were very upset
that, they were some how
responsible for our relationship.

They weren't.
I was a mess of the largest
messiest sort.

Many calls to the police
and trips into court
before this marriage
was fully laid to rest.

BELIEFS..

298

The court made us go to counseling
before we could proceed with the divorce.
We agreed to meet
at the office in San Luis Obispo.
When I arrived, he was already there.

The councilor ask who wanted to start?
He said, "I will" Boy did he.
He called me all sorts on names
told how I was frigid,
that I didn't clean,
there was so much he was
angrier and angrier.

Then the councilor asks me
if what he said was true?
I thought for a second,

"It really doesn't matter
if it's true or not,
he believes it"

The councilor said to him,
"I believe you hate women"
"I further believe you
should get a divorce."

Well now he got to see the person
I had lived with.
He almost came over the desk
after the poor guy.

"He said, you're a marriage counselor
you aren't supposed to tell people
to get a divorce."

I ask If I could please leave

and if they could keep him here
until I got to my car.

I got a head start,
but I guess they couldn't
make him stay there.

He was some ways behind me
he kept saying,
"Stop right there,
stop right there,
do you hear me,
I said Stop"

I cut him off in mid-sentence,
"I don't ever have to
listen to a word you say ever again."
He got a strange look on his face.
I got to my car unlocked it and got in.

"He said, you are so sexy right now"
I shook my head,
he could not have said that?
I started my car and drove away.

We divorced—
which was another ordeal.
Crazy thing is—
he tells everyone we split up
because I cheated on him.
I get asked if it's true.
I always say, "Yes".

Why do I have to learn
so many things the hard way?

God saved me from some terrible disease,

from running into trouble with the law.
I figured I could so easily have derailed
His plan for me,
which made my next thoughts
even more horrendous.

I had decided that I hadn't gained
anything but heartache,
by trying to be a Christian.

I decided to do whatever I pleased,
without a moral compass.

I can look back now and see someone
I just didn't know at all.
I had been stripped of every shred of myself.
I had no me anymore.

I am beyond thankful every day,
that God did not allow me
to be corrupted by this world.
It broke His heart, but he waited,
quietly kept calling me back,
to his unending love and forgiveness.

It is an awful,
and a wonderful day—
to be able to drop to your knees,
and just give it all up to God.

There was shame,
and the lifting of burden at the same time.
Being the human that I am,
I still take myself to task frequently,
about what a wretched sinner I am,
only because of the
covering of the blood of Jesus,

can my God even look at me.

At the same time,
I am condemned,
I can see me
running into God's arms someday,
because His word is Alive, Active,
and True today and always,
even if mine isn't.

He *is* my Father.
I never knew the love of a father,
but my spirit knows God's Love.

GUILY BUT PARDONED...

Oh, but "if" this were the end of the bad,
and the total return to the right path.

I had an abortion about 4 weeks later.

I once again put myself on the other side
the divide I had constructed.

Never, I would never!
How many times had I stood up and said,
"I would *never*."
My word is worthless.
God forgive me.

I closed my heart and did it.
I was ashamed that I got pregnant out-of-wedlock.
I was making excuses all over the place,
overwhelmed that I had three little ones already,
ones that I felt I was a terrible mother to.
I was just going to hide this sin from the world.

I broke my God's heart again.
I was down to the point of just dying,

I called my mom.

I was crying,
I told her how terrible I was,
how unforgivable it was.

"You *murderer*!
You are the spawn of Satan,
you are not my daughter,
you murderer!"

She was still screaming at me
when I hung up the phone.

I knew I should just raise my children
as best I could and find hell in the end.

I cried until I had no tears,
no sound came out,
only a contorted face of eternal agony.

The PTL club program came on TV.
I started to turn it off,
then decided
to call their number.

This amazing woman of God,
whom I know I shall be able to thank someday,
gave me hope again.

Romans 7:7-24 talks of man's sinful nature,
          a slave to the law of sin.
Romans 8:1 says, "Therefore, because of our sinful nature,
          there is now no condemnation for those who are in Christ
Jesus,
          because through Christ Jesus, the law of the Spirit of Life
set me free
          from the law of sin and death."

The rest of that whole chapter is a miracle salve
that has healed me and freed me time and time again.
I now start with the "Renewing of my mind,
the giving my life over to the guidance of the Spirit."

An extra gift that God gave me,
is complete and total forgiveness—
I can give it to those who have hurt me, and I have hurt.
I try to remember to assign good motives to people,
which is contrary to how I usually worked.

################

There are seasons in this life,
I was born
had a mom
became a mom
with a daughter of my own.

This event changed my feelings
about my mom
about myself also.

I look back and forward
to place myself in the daughter
and the mother place.

My feelings toward my mom
toward my daughter
to myself in each place
have changed and grown.

Things that I felt about my mom
that I hope my daughter
doesn't feel about me.
The way my daughter appears to me
I don't want to be or appear to my mother.
My heart is calmed and churned by this new sight.
I can now see clearer
know that it took time and changing of seasons
for me to get to this place
to grant Grace and Mercy to my daughter
as she goes along her own road
and to myself as I work out my relationship
with my mother,
to my mother that she might be blissfully unaware.
I now see it easier to forgive
let things go,

when I see my daughter will
come to the same place of need
and understanding someday I can be patient,
after all she is her mother's daughter.

###############

PARTING OF WAYS...

My step dad was now a single man.
He stayed with my mom some 18 years,
til finally he could not take it anymore.

When he finally left for good,
the girls cried and were hugging him.
The baby that I had met for the first time
when we left the orphanage,
was about to get a shock.

Mom was in lash out mode.
"He's not even your father"

I assumed that my dad
was her dad.
Dad was stunned
that mom would be so mean.

I was shocked too.

"Why would you do this to her?"
Dad was close to tears, sadness & anger
pushed each other to get first place.

I don't know if my sister asked
or if she thought mom was just being mean.

Years later mom told her,
her father was another person.
My sister searched and found
her father and a grandmother.

It was like a dream I had had forever.
But, I wanted to be totally adopted though.

Dad was not an innocent in the mix,
although I think,

to use a term that applied to him,
the "deck was stacked against him."
He was a gruff,
but oh-so-lovable,
big man,
not given to yard work
or manual labor--period.
He hated for my mom to mow the lawn,
because people would think badly of him.
He had no intention of mowing the lawn,
even if it grew nine feet tall.

My mom would get mad,
"Am I supposed to wait till it's dark?"
She would storm out and mow it extra-good.
Dad would be shaking mad,
red-faced, and storm after her.

"HIRE someone, expletive, expletive, expletive."
Funny-- I guess he thought the neighbors
couldn't hear him or something.

I think he was afraid they might think badly of him
because she was doing the yard work.
The older ones of us had already left home,
it was just the three girls at home.

My Dad would not allow them
to do this kind of thing.
Yes, is the answer to the question,
were they screwed up.

My Mom still stalked him—
even after he left.
She would go to the poker room
and make a scene.

It got to where the regulars
were afraid to go there.

It made my mom so mad
anytime someone said,
"I'm afraid of her."
She was completely blown away
that anyone could possibly
be afraid of her.
Why?

I had thought that my mom
would get happy
when they split up.
She always made you believe
it was someone else's fault—
never hers.

She moved for some time to Oregon.
I had encouraged her
to take herself out of this area
and maybe she would feel better not seeing him
She moved.

I don't know if that was good for her or not.
My two youngest sisters
went with her.

PLANTING, WEEDING ...HARVESTING?

Dad lived in town,
played poker every night,
he lived like a slob.
He didn't "do cleaning."

I got him to meet me for lunch one day,
we had a talk about what I was doing
what he was doing,
then he looked down at me and said,
"I know I was a terrible father to you.

Can we do something about that?"
He looked like he was in so much pain,
his eyes were welling up.

"Dad, there's nothing we can do
about the past."
He looked shocked and sad.

"But - we can start all over.
From this day forward,
you can be the best dad ever."

He bundled me up in his big old bear hug,
we both cried in front of Taco Bell.
I started to go to clean his house
once a week,
my sister would go in between,
the two of us loved him up,
we both had chatted with him
many times, about
giving his life to the Lord.

It was a slow process
because he had such self-loathing.
He had such a painful
and terrible childhood,

going hungry,
doing literally anything
to eat.

We never realized until later,
that what we thought was a jolly big man,
hated himself daily.

It finally made sense to me,
why he would react like he did
about the kids being hungry.
I don't think he even realized this truth.

What joy it was,
when one day,
my dad went to pick up my kids
from school for me,
because I was tied up at work.

The joy came when they told me
how fun grandpa King was.
My heart just was full-to-overflowing.
They went to McDonald's,
had lunch,
and back to the house
where he watched TV with them—
kid shows even.

I believe he was happier with himself then,
if that could be possible.
I made it a point to get over to his
little apartment, and clean for him,
trim his hair and beard.
Then he would try to pay me,
I'd let him take me to lunch.

Like I said, He was a slob,

but he didn't care.
He liked clean,
but not done by him.

Dad lived at the beach for a while
he loved to temperature and the salt air.
Then my little sister was coming back to California,
from Oregon with her new baby girl.
So, dad decided to move back to Atascadero,
get a place big enough for them to stay with him.

He tried to the best of his ability,
it was hard for both of them,
the baby too.
His heart was in the right place,
his skills in this area
were sadly lacking.

My sister and I both talked
to him about giving his heart to Jesus.
He would always say
he had done too much bad,
God couldn't forgive him.
I told him,
I'm sure my sister did too,
that he was wrong.

We serve a Big God,
He has already paid the price
for every sin forever
with His Son's own blood,
just take the Gift.

Not this time--maybe next.
"Don't wait too long, dad."

I went to see him one day, my day off,

he was in an odd mood.
He looked at me and said,

"I could take you to bed in a heartbeat."

"What?" I was stunned.
"Dad! What are you thinking?"
"We're not really related you know,
it wouldn't be wrong."

"WHAT?
Dad, you know what has happened in my life,
how messed up I've been,
how could you say this?

You are my DAD,
and you will act like my dad.
Stop these thoughts and be my dad."

"Ok" he said. "Are we Ok?"

Yes - we are Ok.
This never happened, and it will never happen again!
I was really shook up by this whole exchange,
I didn't let him know how much.

I still can be non-reactionary to the most
inappropriate acts or shocking words.

Some kind of a crazy coping skill or something.
It happens fast, and without too much thought on my part,
Inward chaos outward calm.

I was so close to my dad,
I was able to know somehow in my heart
he was a very damaged person.

It was a very difficult day.
I cleaned and went home.
No beard or haircut,
no lunch.

I got in my car,
pulled out of his driveway,
and cried all the way home.

WORKING OUT MY WORTH

I was working two jobs.
One was my cleaning company--cleaning.
I had started doing house cleaning,
which progressed to offices,
then commercial jobs.

I even began to bid State contracts,
I ended up getting every contract
I bid on for some ten years.

The other job was at a car lot.
I wanted to sell cars,
don't ask me why.

My future husband was jealous
of the salesmen at the car lot.
One morning I was getting ready for work
he walked in,
"You're not wearing that underwear to work."
"What?
Are you kidding?"
"No, I'm not kidding!"

Later that day he called
And boy was he mad
"Are you wearing underwear?"
I had taken off the ones
he didn't want me to wear
and put them into his lunchbox.

"You told me not to,
sorry I gotta go."
I hung up and laughed.

I had told tell him
sales men were no threat to him.

Prior to when I married for the second time,
it turned out that I had a tumor on my thyroid
which needed to be removed.
I was unsure what to do,
no insurance, and little money.

My future husband, said,
"It will totally ruin you to have this surgery,
you will be financially ruined for life!"
"Oh no, what am I going to do?"

He hemmed and hawed a moment,
as though the perfect idea came to him,
he said, "Well, we were going
to get married eventually,
we might as well do it now,
you'll have insurance."

I was so sure he was right—
not about the getting married part—
but the ruined part.

I was ruined alright,
but not financially.
He pretty much picked up
where the last guy left off.

Trying to blend a family is difficult,
who has those skills?

I had started to clean houses
to make some money.
That led to cleaning offices.
I had an ad in the yellow pages
I got more business than I could do.

The State hospital mailed out bid packets

to every local janitorial company.
When It came I opened it and looked at it
then right into the trash can.

I told my husband when he came home.
He pulled it out of the trash.
"Why don't you try to figure
what you want per hour,
how many hours it might take,
whatever supplies you would need."

There was going to be a walk through that next week.
I decided I would try to figure out if I could do it.
I was almost overwhelmed as we
entered through the sally port.

One door shut loudly and the other one opened.
There were "patients" everywhere.
I kept referring to them as prisoners.
It was a mental hospital,
guards armed with tasers,
they weren't supposed to use on the "patients".

There were bars on every window.
There were 40 window panes in each frame,
each pane was 4"X8".
All the squeegees had to be cut to size.
I counted the window frames as we went along,
decided how long each pane might take
did some multiplication.
The ceilings in the hallways were 30 feet high,
just the same I felt claustrophobic.

I had to figure out how to reach the ceilings,
the contract called for cleaning windows
and everything above 8 feet.
The hallways were 1/4-mile one way

1/3 mile the other way.

The place was huge.
I figure it would talk about 15 days.
The kitchen flues were a huge part also
they were larger than
commercial or Industrial.
You could get a minivan up there.

We could climb all the way up to clean.
The top of the flue had bars.
There were several dining rooms
We were supposed to clean the walls and ceiling.
The patients though it was a cool game
to throw butter pats to the ceiling tiles.
We spent a lot of time to get them all down.

I won the bid on this contract
9 out of 11 times.
Partly, at least because
I was a woman owned business,
that gave priority points.

I had to commit to use 1%
of the contract in completing the contract.
I had to order cleaning rags
from a Veteran owned business,
which cost at least
4 time what I would have paid locally.

I bought a 5-gallon container of
Windex
409 concentrates,
eight squeegees
a shop vac.,
extension poles
and duster heads for them.

I rented a rolling in scaffolding.
I had to order my business cards
from veteran owned business.
I enclosed 1 card with my contract.

The total from veteran owned businesses was a $150.00.
Nowhere near the 1 percent I needed.
My bid came in 30K less than the next bid.
They gave me the contract,

I made a good faith effort.
Trying to find somewhere to waste
at least, $800 more dollars.
No luck, I didn't need anything else.

It took 15 days to get through
the whole place with 8 employees.
The first contract was $47,000.00
the last time was $86,000.00
for the exact same job.

The first time I was in the laundry area,
I felt light headed.
I walked around trying to figure out what I would need.
There were shelved of men's underwear labeled,
Small, Medium. Large, X Large.
I saw the same thing for T-shirts
pants, shirts, socks.

There were institutional sized washers and dryers.
It was steamy, I couldn't breathe.
I told them I needed to
go get a drink in the hallway.

What was wrong with me?
Then it occurred to me,
it was an orphanage memory

all these years later.

The business was going really well.
King Klean Janitorial had a great reputation
I had successfully bid 3 state contracts to date.

PREGNANT PAUSE FOR TWO

We were married about 5 years
when my husband decided
he wanted a baby.
I just didn't want to
go through a pregnancy again.

Delivery, body stretching,
diapers and all the stuff of babies again.
How would I do my business?

I tried to tell him there are 26 sets
of twins in our family at this time,
I have twin uncles for god sake.
Over 30 years old
3 or more kids already
= TWINS.

My sort of, mother in law
said she wanted a grandchild too.
I wanted a girl every time.
I had boy and a boy and a boy.
All beautiful boys.
I gave up on a girl at that point.

I finally gave in,

I of course got pregnant immediately.

I was so sick I could barely lift my head
off the living room floor.
I went for my first o b appointment, the doctor said,
"let's have an ultrasound done"
Ok I thought whatever.

He gave his nurse the order and said,
"Tell them it's to rule out twins."
"Wait, what?

What are you saying?"
"Don't worry you are bigger
then you should be at this point,
we need to find out
how far along you really are"
He signed the chart,
gave it to the nurse and looked at me
"They can get you in this morning can you make it?"

I had the boys with me.
I did want to find out a due date,
the four of us went to the hospital.

The ultra sound tech said
the boys could just
sit in the chairs by the wall
while she did her measurements.

The littlest one
was standing in the chairs
crawling under the chairs
jumping off the chairs.

All I could do was glare at him
if
he looked my way.

"Oh my" the tech said,
"That's the second set of twins today"
What?
"What did you say?" -
 she pointed to the screen
"when you see the beep it's a heartbeat"
She moved the thing over my stomach and sure enough,
"Beep Beep"

"You can't just say that to a person"

"it's not the second set of twins for me"
I looked at the boys and I was just stunned.
"Mom, are we getting two babies?"
Two babies oh my goodness.

I went to the fire department to tell my husband.
One of the other firefighters said,
"What is it triplets?"
"No",
"just twins"

My husband slowly started
to slide down the wall to a seated position.
"April Fools?"

"No" I said flatly.

"We don't have room for twins"

"We" don't have room for twins? "
I, don't have room for twins."
I can't believe this is happening.
After the shock wore off,
I thought I might get my girl!

I wanted her to be Kaci Marie.
My mother in law on her death bed ask,
"If one of them is a girl
will you name her Megan?"
Of course, I would.

I hoped there were two girls Kaci and Megan.
The last four months were mostly in the hospital.
I could not have sworn with certainty
I even had feet or that my shoes matched.
75 pounds I gained.

They were 7lbs15oz. & 7lbs 2 oz.
It was very hard,
I sucked at it miserably.
The doctor said,
it appeared I was originally
carrying 3 babies.
Triplets?

When I was waiting to have
each of my children
I prepared a bag,
the first time -with the things that
I was told I would need.

Baby clothes, hard candy, robe etc.
After 5 hours labor,
I had my first son.
I was exhausted
couldn't get out of bed
till the next day.

The second child
I needed less
and different things,
my previous experience
taught me that a newborn outfit
could be a tee shirt and diaper.

No need for some outfit that was going to be way to big
and end up being covered with that black stool
that didn't come out in the wash.

After 3 hours labor, boy number 2 arrived,
20 minutes later I walked down the hallway
to the nursery to look in the window
with the rest of the family.

The third child
I took my own night gown
figured it would be 20 minutes or so.

My doctor this time was very
new at being a doctor.
With each contraction
blood would gush.
The doctor actually panicked
right in front of me.

This very tall white-haired woman
appeared in the door way.
She walked over and said let me take a look.
She said next contraction
honey push this baby out.

I did just that.
It was 8 hours start to finish
son number 3 made his entrance.
I cooed over him and
gave him to his daddy –
while I took a well-deserved nap.
I had this down,
no surprises –
eeerrrkk! wait –

This little guy was jaundice –
turns out his numbers were 18 ¾
a baby is usually transfused at 20.
He was under the lights in an incubator
for about a week before he could come home.
What a shakeup that was.
So, three lovely sons – but no girl
….what to do?

BABIES..

After much encouragement
another long hot summer,
July arrived and with that – TWINS.
Boy number 4, calm and sleepy,
followed by a very mad little girl,
now my joy was complete!
By C-section –
7lbs 15 oz and 7lbs 2oz .

Much harder to get around after that little party!
Needless to say after that –
it was ♫ Always never the same ♫ –
around our very full,
always in the kitchen,
loud and child filled home.
Thank you, Lord

I can look back now
and know I had post-partum depression.
I had a c- section,
I was nursing two babies
on different schedules,
I was sleep deprived.
Plus, I still had 3 boys
who needed their mom too.

One morning I was unable
to get myself to a good place.
The twins were in their bassinets
they were both crying.

I screamed at the top of my lungs,
"Shut Up"
Their dad came through the door at that point.

"You don't yell at babies!"
I walked around him and out to the patio.

He came out and said,
"They are still crying"
"yes, but if you close the door
I can't hear them"

He made a few more comments
went into the living room
turned up the tv
he couldn't hear them either.
When I was calm
I went back in
took both of them
into the bedroom and nursed them.
That always calmed me down too.
They were drifting off to sleep
I changed them and
laid them in the crib together.
I wish I could say that
it was smooth sailing after that
that I stayed calm.
Twins are not easy.

I loved that they were twins.
I loved that they were so adorable.
I loved to dress them similar.
I loved when they slept.

Keeping two toddlers in
bed at night turned out to be impossible.
We would wake up with them
in our bed morning
after morning.

Their dad wanted to put
chicken wire over their cribs –
I think he was kidding.

We decided to lock our bedroom door
and tell them they couldn't get in.
I opened the door in the morning
they were asleep on the rug outside our door.

Meg had her thumb in her mouth
and the corner of her blankey,
Trav was covered with the rest of her blankey.
I tried to sleep in the floor by their bed
to keep them in their bed.
I woke up in the floor
with them cuddled next to me,
It took a long time to finally get them
to make use of their own beds.
I was frequently overwhelmed
trying to run a household with 5 kids.
Laundry was impossible.
The pile that would be in the
laundry room floor
was staggering.
Then folding!

I was trying to fold laundry
I like everything to be folded perfectly.
Sheets had to be undistinguishable,
whether fitted or flat.

I had two big stacks of towels
all neatly folded.
The boys were wrestling around
knocked the towel over into the floor.

I went from mom
to a banshee in 1.36 seconds!
I was screaming and crying
having the biggest pity party ever.

As I was telling them
how they were driving me crazy,
I realized Megan
had crawled up on the couch
singing over and over,
"Let the peace of God rule in your heart"
it took 3 times of her softly singing in my ear
before my brain noticed.

I was stunned.
I hugged her up,
told her thank you.
God is so good.

I told the boys I was sorry
ask if they would please
help me fold laundry
and put it away.

They all helped.
In my very marked up bible,
Colossians 3:13 is highlighted in yellow
has those very words.

"Let the peace of God rule in your heart".
In the margin there is a heart that says,
"Meg" and the year, 1989.
My story so far you can see
I am not perfect,
I do have the tools now,
to know when I've set off in my own way,
which I still do from time to time.
Now I can quickly turn around
back to my Father.

SIBLING SABOTAGE..

For a short while,
we had my husband's sister living with us.
She was a high-functioning,
mentally limited adult.

They figured about an 8-year-old mentality.
She would not talk
unless she had to answer a question
that wasn't a head nod, yes or no.

While the babies were small,
it was like having three infants at times.
She could not get a bra on without some help,
if she had her period,
and there were no feminine products,
she would just not use one.
If there was no toilet paper--same thing.
You get the idea.

She had been able to make her own tea
at her last care home,
and at her aunt's house too.

So, she made her own tea at our house.
One day I noticed a terrible burn on her arm—
a big blister.
I asked her what happened.
She shrugged--no information.

When her brother got home, I told him,
he asked her, did you burn it on the tea-pot?
She said, yes
I told him, "no more tea-pot!"
He had a fit.

He gave her the answer,
Who knows how she got the burn.

But, no teapot it is.

"How could I say that?
She had tea every night for some 30 years."
"She will have to use the microwave, or no tea."
We finally settled on the microwave,
which she picked up real fast.

Unfortunately, my husband found it
necessary to intercede,
for her constantly
feeling he needed to protect her
from me.

I asked her one night
if she wanted salad dressing,
she said, "no".

Her brother ask why she didn't have salad dressing.
"She didn't want any."
Why was he looking to see if she had salad dressing?

He turned to her and said,
"Did Ty ask you if you wanted salad dressing?"
-why would he think
I wouldn't give her salad dressing?

She answered," No" ..very clearly.
"Ok," I thought.
"What do we have here?"

There began to be more and more friction.
The other kids would turn the channel,
my husband would have a fit.
I felt angry to have this whole situation in our house.

"Debby was watching that."

She would just watch whatever was on
didn't really seem to care one way or the other.

I told the kids to just ask her
if you may turn the channel.
She would always say "no" to them and laugh.

But if I asked if I could turn it,
she would just shake her head "no."
She didn't really care if it was turned.
I told her she could watch for an hour
then someone else got to pick.

There just got to be constant problems
with her brother trying to defend her
or protect her somehow.
It would end with the boys being sent to bed
with him yelling at them.

I went to check on her in the shower one morning,
the tub was almost full of dirty water.
I had asked, then told her,
not put the stopper down when she showered.
I saw red!
I opened the shower door
slapped her on the butt like she was 6 years old or something.
I pulled up the stopper and told her I had enough of this.
"You can understand I don't want you to put the plug in? Right?"
She shook her head "yes."

"Well, why in the world do you insist on doing it?"

She smiled and shrugged.
This situation had to change—
obviously, I was out of control.

My anger was building,

it wasn't just toward her,
but she was not safe here.
I knew something had to change.
I finally had enough,

I tried to get my husband to understand
the difficulty this was causing me with two babies.
He wasn't going to make any changes.

I told him that either she goes,
or I do.
He gave me no choice

We went to a counselor,
of course, my husband told him
what I said, and the counselor said,

"We're not here to determine
what's best for you or your wife,
we're here to determine
what's best for your sister."

"Hold on there a minute."
I stood up.
"I want it to be clear to everyone
if you decide that the best thing for her
is to live at our home,
she will be living alone with her brother,
I will not be there."

She went to a care home
with other gals her age and ability.
We had been getting about
$900 a month to keep her
plus living expenses,
which turned out to be the biggest reason
my husband wanted her there,

but his guilt, or something,
made all our lives miserable.

Relative residue remains

Now I had non-stop reference to
my cold heartedness
my lack of compassion.
"She is 'your' sister,
your own aunt told you on her death-bed
do not to bring her here to live.

But all you could see was her money. "
"Hey, we took care of her not for the money!
Well, not for the money,
but it was right for her to pay her expenses."

"We,
did not take care of her.
I took care of her."

She's a girl,
I couldn't do it-
He said, like I was crazy to not recognize that.

It took a long time for this banter to stop.

On holidays he would come in and say,
"Would you mind too terribly
if my sister came over?
I mean it won't
ruin your day or anything?"
He would never ever forgive this.

I started hearing from him like a broken record.
"I'm sorry - I forgot –
it's not my fault." mocking me.
I seemed to be constantly defending myself
over all kinds of crazy stuff.
If I cleaned the kitchen, he would blow up.

"Why don't you have these lazy slugs in there doing the dishes,

instead of them sitting on the couch watching TV?"
He would go in the living room
grab them up by an arm and drag them to the kitchen.

"I can clean my own kitchen if I want to!"
He would storm back in the kitchen,
yell in my face,
while poking his finger
on the end of my nose.
"Don't say I didn't try to help you."

Back in the living room he went and
turned up the sound of the ball game.
Oh, that was it.
He wanted to watch the game
and couldn't just ask or turn the channel.

The kids helped me with the kitchen,
then we went in their room to watch TV.
The twins came in the bedroom with us,
we were laughing at some funny video show,
when my husband stormed to the bedroom door
and slammed it.
We all jumped.
"Guess we were too loud,
or too happy."

DESPAIR, DREAMS & HOPE

I had a dream and it was so real,
I woke up crying.
I dreamed that God told me that
my dad would come to Him,
and my husband would go to church.
I was so happy.

Wow, my dad is going to become a Christian.
I felt in my bones that it was true.
I told my husband,
he wasn't even sarcastic or anything.
He seemed to just ponder the idea and said,
"That's great about your dad."
I didn't notice till later,
that he'd left himself out of it.

I talked to my dad that night on the phone
I told him I would be over
To see him in the morning
and spend the day.

I told him I loved him so much,
He said he loved me too.
I had worked 6 a.m. to 7.p.m. that day,
I was exhausted and immediately fell into a deep sleep.
My husband woke me up around 10,
to say my dad was going to the hospital,
he asked if I wanted to go?

"No, he's ok."
I was so tired I could barely talk.
Again, my husband woke me up and said,
"Honey, your dad is gone."

I fought to wake up,
"He's at the hospital,
remember?"

"No -Ty he's gone.

He died as soon as he got to the hospital."

My brain was fuzzy,
I was so confused.
"What did you say?"
"No, no, no, he's OK.
He just went to the hospital.
I have to go see him."
I got out of bed,
grabbed the car keys,
headed for the door.

"You're wearing a T-shirt."
"I don't care--I have to see him.
"This is not true,
oh God my dad's in hell."
I was, all of a sudden,
overcome with terrible grief.
"Why hadn't I tried harder
to get my dad to believe."

My husband put his arm around
my waist very gently, and said,
"Ty, look at me."
I stopped and turned to face him.

"Remember your dream?"
"What?"
"Your dream, that your dad would go to God
 I would go to church?
Your dad's in heaven,
God told you he was."

"Why now?"
We were doing so well, why now?

I remember someone told me once,
that sometimes God takes a person like my dad,
at the first opportunity
because he's as good as he can get in this life.
I don't know if that is true. Crazy!

It took a long time for me to realize
that God said my husband would "go to church,"
which means a building, not a savior.
I could not believe something could hurt this much.
I missed my dad like part of me was ripped out.

I was in total despair, with some hope also.

#############

Bridges span small spaces and large ones.
Bridges can be a log or tons of steel.
Some bridges will stand forever, and others rot away.
We oft times need to cross bridges,
sometimes burn them –
hopefully we don't burn the wrong ones
not while standing in the middle of them.
I can see those who first came up with bridges,
hmmm, what a gulf?
How can we get to the other side?
Probably a wise old white-haired lady
was giving good counsel to a soul in need,
"Build a bridge and get over it" – Eureka!
That's it!
we will find a way to get
the two sides closer,
somehow.

If we cooperate with those
on the other side of the gulf
build slowly upon the ground, we have –
we will meet at some point.
The middle maybe.
But people's talents and
ambitions are different,
the work put down by one
can be supported and
increased by another and another.

Each one that adds is of value,
all will be part of the whole,
each adds to those before and
those who come after.

The Cross was the work of one man,
He worked to the completion of the purpose
for which He was sent.

It cost His human body,
which he obediently laid down,
to save our souls

Spark the Spirit within us again.
Before the Cross there was
a great gulf between man and God.

The Cross spans that unspanable distance,
we can now draw near
to the Father through His Son,
by way of the Cross
which supported our Lord
as He took upon Himself
all the sins of the world,

Past, Present & Future.
That old serpent still tries
to tell us from time to time,
"Oh, that sin wasn't covered" or
"That sin is Way too big for God to forgive"

"Remember when you did this or that?"
He is the head liar,
he cannot tell the truth.
I trust God's Word!

Jesus is the WORD,
He has saved us,
past tense,
we are saved.

The Word (Jesus)
is the Light (Jesus)
Where the Light is there is NO darkness.
Be filled with the Light (Jesus)
keep God's Word (Jesus) ever in your heart,
then speak what the heart is full.

Just go share your Light (Jesus)
with those who are stuck in the dark
unable to find the bridge,
show them the Way (Jesus).
God is not slow to bring judgement
to the world as men might think,

No – He is patient that all
have a chance to answer His call
and accept the sacrifice made for us all –
that none should perish
but all attain eternal life in Heaven.

All that to say,
Dad had crossed that bridge
and was fully in the light!

****

BIG THINGS IN SMALL BOXES...

The things that have to be done in the world
to help us let go still had to be done.

Dad always told us
he was going to leave money for all of us kids.
He made it a point that
I would be in charge of passing it out.

We always believed him,
never really thought about it on a regular basis.

We still had to pick out a coffin for his body.
He had told every single one of us,
that he was to be buried
in the cheapest pine box they had.
He made us all promise.

So, it was me, and one or two brothers and sisters,
that went to the funeral home to pick out,
"The Box."

It was awful.
I told the man,"
He wants the cheapest wooden box you have."
It felt awful to even say the words.

The poor man went in the back and rolled out
a Dracula coffin--just like on TV.

It was awful.
What did we do?
We all laughed.

I told the poor man,
"that's the one."
How awful.
We left there,

I felt just terrible.

This just feels disrespectful.
Why had my dad not felt like he deserved
the things that would mark his leaving
and allow us to show respect.
It wasn't long before the guy
at the funeral home called me at home.
"Mrs. King, I don't want to be indelicate,
but your dad won't fit in the box."

"What?" "The box is too small"
I laughed again,
"Ok, well then let's go with
the least expensive next step up."
"After all, he can't get mad now,
we tried."

What the heck
he's not going to get mad anyway.
The poor man offered to let me
come down and see our father,
with his shoulders rolled forward,
trying to fit in that cheap box,
but this made me laugh too.

Don't ask me why it was so funny,
but as I described the scene to each of my siblings,
they laughed too.

SOMETHINGS DON'T CLEAN UP....

We went and cleaned out my dad's apartment.
My husband and I arrived first,
then the rest of them slowly filed in too.
We took out so much junk,
things that a daughter doesn't want to find of her dad's—
enough said on that.
We did find thousands of dollars
in uncashed military retirement checks.
My little sister would have been his beneficiary.
We took them home to call the army to see what to do.

Anyway, we cleared it out,
cleaned it up.
It took a long time to finally get finished.
I was the last one there
I backed out the door
looked around one last time.
I shut the door and locked it.

The funeral was Friday.
All six of us kids were there,
and mom too.

My poor little sister broke down so badly,
yelling at him,
that he had told her
he would always be there for her.
It was just surreal.

We had placed some poker chips
in his pocket and fixed his hair.
I was shocked that his beard was so cold,
he looked like
he would just open his eyes at any moment,
this would just be a terrible joke.

That evening I got a call,

all the siblings were going to meet at
my sister's house to pow-wow –
NO spouses allowed.

I could not imagine what it was about.
I thought maybe they just wanted
to say a private farewell.

When I arrived, they were all already there.
I was talking to my older brother.
He had been gone a long time,
just came back for the funeral.
My brothers didn't have much of
a relationship with our stepfather.

I was really glad they came,
even if it was just so we could all be together.
I told them that the military had said
they would not let my sister have
any of the uncashed checks.
They would be sending her
a small amount as a death benefit.

The night ended with something ugly.
Greed and anger were front and center.
The devil had made his way into our day.
I told them all I loved them so much,
some responded.

I told God I needed to not let
anything grow from this.
I ask him to help me let it go.
I walked out of that house,
I was not Ok.

My husband had wanted to go back in there
to do something.

I don't know why he listened to me,
but he didn't go in.

REPAIRING AND DESTROYING....

I was completely to the end of my rope.
All the things that I had experienced
throughout my life
this was finally the thing that
pushed me into counseling.
I believe it changed my whole life,
in a way I'm grateful to my family.

It took about five years to work through everything
"soup to nuts,"
but I got healthy for the first time in my life.
I learned that I had choices,
that I didn't have to worry about what people thought,
that I was a good and valuable human being,
that it was ok for me to love my children,
that they were not a punishment.

And finally, I learned that I serve a big God.
My current relationship was toxic—
I had made so much effort to work things out.
Sometimes it is just not possible.

Don't get into a relationship
when you don't yourself or the other person.
I needed to know me.

Eventually I decided that God
would take care of me,
I left my husband, who had
quite stolen my joy.
He was by now literally
a falling-down drunk.

He would pull his truck into the driveway,
open his door,
fall partway out,
pass out in the driveway,

where I would leave him.

Most nights, when he would get home,
the kids saw him pull into the driveway,
they would all get up and say goodnight
head for their rooms.

He got up on Saturday morning
laid on the couch saying he was sick,
someone needed to make him something to eat.
I walked outside and pulled weeds,
but my little daughter made him some soup.

He came falling into the house one night
said he was hungry.
I told him there was leftover dinner in the fridge.
He said he was sick,
couldn't I just make it for him.
No, I said, I was going to bed.

My little girl was so upset,
"Mommy, he is sick, and he's hungry,
you need to make him something."
"He can get it himself, and he's not sick."

She was so upset,
"I'll get you something daddy."
She started to the kitchen, and I stopped her.
"Go to bed."
"I have to get Daddy something to eat,"
she had her lip pushed out and hands on her little hips.

"You go to bed, I'll take care of Daddy."
"Fine!"
She went back and kissed him and
went to bed giving me a very dirty look.

He looked up at me and said, "I want eggs."
I laughed a little laugh and said,
"You know where they are."
He called me a bitch, and I went to bed.

At one time,
I had tried to help the kids
have some kind of respect for him—
which was just impossible.

BELIEVING THE UNBELIEVABLE...

I suffered all my life,
wondering how to, as the Bible says,
honor your mother and father.
How was I to do that?
But it doesn't say,
"if" they are nice, and good, or lovable.

It just says, "Honor your father and your mother."
I, for one, don't believe the Bible never is wrong,
I do believe that my thoughts are nowhere near God's thoughts,
this is one thing that he will make me understand some day.

I started to have nightmares.

As a child, I dreamed several times
that a man broke into our apartment
cut a huge X in my back with an enormous knife.
I would go running down the hall,
trying to find my mother.

Finally, I would burst into this apartment
where I saw smoke coming from under the door.

My mom and three other people,
sometimes my aunts and my grandmother,
sometimes strangers, would be playing cards.
I'd run up to the table and
turn around to show them my back.

Each one took a piece of the flesh,
peeled it back, as I went around the table,
when I got to my mother,
she grabbed a big box of salt
poured it in the wound,
then I would wake up.

But, why would these dreams start again now?

I told the counselor
about my whole life,
it was so draining.

I would come home,
just be totally wiped out.
I got my husband to go with me,
he went by himself a few times too.
It was a good idea,
but he just wasn't ready
to make any changes in his life.

I did learn that I should not help him,
as I said earlier,
and to let him suffer his own consequences.
The kids (mostly the twins)
did not understand this at all.

The counselor told me that my mom
had known what was happening with my dad.

"Wait a minute?
No!"
I didn't want to know that –
I had no allies?

"Why would she?
Her little girl?"
She grabbed a box of tissues.
"Ty, she knew."

I was resigned to it,
I let out a hard breath
I accepted it.

This answered a lot—
maybe.

THE FADED FACTS ARE CLEAR...

I was going to go shopping for whatever,
I found myself pulling into her complex.
I would tell my mom that the counselor had said that,
she knew.
I knocked,
she said come in.

She was in her recliner
with some sewing project on her lap.
I ask how she felt
she was in a lot of pain.
I said I'm sorry.
Then I just said it, "mom"
I saw my councilor this week and -
She stopped me
"Oh Pooh, are you still seeing that councilor?"
Yes, mom it's helped me a lot.

"She said that you knew –
knew - what was happening all along"

My Mom jumped up,
"I did not know!"
She was frantically looking for her cordless phone
protesting the whole time.

"I did not know"
She was frantically searching for her cigarettes at the same time.
Finally, she fished the phone out on the recliner somewhere,
"We are calling her right now,
Ty Beth. What's her phone number?"
She was near tears.

"Mom, it doesn't matter what she thinks,
I just wanted to tell you."
She was again frantic, lighting her cigarette.
"Ty Beth, I did not know."

She fell into her big chair
started telling me about how the whole thing
us going to the orphanage
wasn't her fault,
that she was lied about then too.

"Eva and Wayne got that -pastor"
she spat that word out like it was bitter as lemons.
"They lied to him
He wrote a letter saying I wasn't a fit mother, all lies!"
"I still have that letter here somewhere"
she started looking through boxes and drawers.

"Mom, it doesn't matter,
I just wanted to tell you what the councilor, thinks."
I calmed her down as best I could and went home.

She knew.

Now, I was sure she knew,

NOT PROTECTED NOT PROTECTING..

It hurt so badly.
I almost felt as though
I was that little kid again,
left for anybody to do anything to,
and no one to protect her.

More revelation followed,
I continued to see the counselor.
I became more, and more aware,

I was reliving my hurts,
magnifying every hurt my kids had,
until I was sure that I was letting them down,
not protecting them.

I projected my enormous pain
on every little disappointment
they experienced.
I didn't want to see them miss anything in life.
I thought they were,
but they weren't.

The things that were part of my life,
purely by the grace of God,
have made me a person of great worth
to his kingdom – I will use this worth for him.
Everybody goes through things.
Some like my mom,
are forever victims of their past
and use it to guide their future.

I had regular altercations with my husband.
It seemed like he needed to make sure I knew
just how stupid I was,
how terribly I had screwed up.

I went to the store,

he had asked me to pick him up some –
some size? some kind? of screws.
I was rushing around to get the things I needed,
to get back home,
so he wouldn't be angry
that he was left with the kids.

When I got back to the house,
he came up to the back door,
"Where's my screws?"

My mom had just arrived
walked down the drive way.
"Oh, no."
I had forgotten,

"Oh man, I forgot."
"I forgot, I forgot!"
He was seething at me,
in my face with his finger,
poking me on the end of my nose.

"You get back in the car
and go get them
now!"

Mom was saying, "Hey"
we hadn't even noticed.
She stepped up and told him,
"you want the screws,
go get them yourself –

Ty has said, "I'm sorry five times at least!

Mind your own business
he went to get his screws.

"Why do you let him treat you like this?
Divorce him!"
she was headed back to her car.

Thanks mom, I said barely audibly.

He came back with the screws
was livid,
still mad
if not madder now.

"Your mother is not welcome here, EVER"
He threw the hardware store bag on the patio,
he wanted to make sure
I fully understood what he was ordering

IN A CORNER. OUT OF REACH.

I just backed up into the house.
I tried to close the door behind me,
but he kept coming.
I continued to back up through the house,
with him pressing the whole way.
I got to the bathroom,
ran in,
and locked the door.

He was so mad,
he was yelling and beating on the door.
I had my hands over my ears and was crying.
"What are you crying like a baby for?
Get out here now!"

I just stood with my back to the sink
hoped the door would hold.
It got quiet,
I decided he had given up and gone outside.

I unlocked the door,
turned the knob,
the whole thing hit me hard.
It broke one of my fingers,
I fell to my knees in pain and fear.

"Let me see it."
I held my hand to my chest,
not wanting him to touch me.

"This isn't my fault, it's your fault.
You should have opened
the door like I told you,
this wouldn't have happened."

I stayed on the floor
didn't answer anything he said.

"If you're not going to let me see it,
then get up and come out of there."

He stormed out of the bedroom
out the back door with a loud slam,
I heard his truck start.

I got up and went to look out the window
to see if he was gone.
I taped up my finger and took some aspirin.

The next time I saw the counselor.

I told her, what happened—
that, it was my fault
for being in the way of the door,
he didn't mean to break my finger,
that I just couldn't seem to remember stuff,
she just sat and looked at me.

"Ty, who was outside the bathroom door?"
"What?"
I was totally thrown.
Wasn't she listening to me?
"My husband," I said,
I shook my head.

"No, Ty.
Who was outside the bathroom door?"
"I told you, my husband."
"No, Ty.   It is your father."
she stopped
looked at me for a moment,
I just stared.
"What?"

I was really confused,

at the same time
had a terrible fear.

"Ty, when your father molested you,
didn't you go lock yourself in the bathroom?"
 I felt like I might faint,
I started to cry,
I was so mad.

"Ty, your father has backed you through the house
into the bathroom for 38 years.
You have to stay out of the bathroom
stop him from ever doing this again."

I didn't answer.
I just sat there
I believed
I could never get out of that bathroom.
It was about a month later,
that we had this lady who had
helped a lot of women
with the same sort of pasts as mine.
She came to our church to teach us
some skills to break free forever.

She had me close my eyes,
she asked me where I was.

"In the bathroom," I said.
"Why are you in the bathroom?"
I started to open my eyes.
"No, Ty.
Stay in the bathroom."
I closed my eyes again.
I remembered the councilor saying
stay out of the bathroom

"Who is outside the door?"
I felt silly.
"My dad?"

I only guessed this because
the councilor had said it to me before.
"Look around the bathroom.
Who else is in there with you?"
In my mind, I looked.
"No one is here but me,"
"Ty.

Isn't Jesus right there with you?"
"NO." I didn't even hesitate.
"I'm all alone."
"Ty, is there a window?"
"Yes."
"Ok, take Jesus' hand,
let him pull you through the window."

I started to have tears slowly escape my eyes.
"He can't."
She touched my knee, I jumped.
"Ty, he can pull you out,
take his hand."

I was so sad,
"He can't."
"The window is very high, and very small."
I felt as though I was
 sinking into the couch that I sat on.

It was something that would happen when
I was just going away to the ceiling
not being part of me.
I opened my eyes.
I didn't want to go away.

She looked at me and seemed disappointed in me.

"Ty, you have to want
to get out of the bathroom."
 I felt like a failure again.
Why wouldn't anybody believe me,
"I can't."

IT CLICKED..

Two days later,
I found myself in the bathroom
my husband once again at the door.
This time, I opened the medicine cabinet,
I searched for some way out.
I was looking at prescription bottles,
nothing was lethal.
Suddenly, I could hear the counselor's words
telling me
get out of the bathroom.

I was overcome with anger.
I had carried a pile of folded towels into the bathroom
sat them on the counter.
I started beating on the towel with every bit of strength
I had and beat all my anger out.
Then I grabbed the door knob,
unlocked the door,
stormed out into his face,

I yelled, shaking and crying,
"You will never do this again.
Don't you ever think you can do this again.
Get out of here!"

He stepped back,
as soon as he got through the bedroom door,
he wrinkled up his nose and said,
"Good God, you're crazy or something."

I looked at him and said,
"Or something"
I wanted to slam the door in his face,
but I didn't want to be behind another door.

Three days later,
I told the counselor about it.

I could barely walk up the stairs to her office,
every muscle in my body hurt.

She told me that I had had
a total adrenaline overload.
I think I started getting a little better after that.
Serious steps were happening.

POSSIBLE EXIT

I was having a terrible time with my moods, .
crying and really being irritable.
I had an appointment for my pap smear in a few weeks,
I figured I would talk to the doctor
then and see what she suggested.
I had been having a period for
ten days at a time,
twice a month
for five years.
The doctor wouldn't do anything,
because I was not anemic.

I was actively trying to work out an exit strategy.
No matter how I worked it,
I was unable to see a way out.
I went for my ob-gyn appointment,
the doctor sent me over for a pelvic ultrasound.
She wouldn't give me any details—
just that I needed to go.
So, I got an appointment for later that week.

Talk about nervous.
It was torture, waiting and wondering.
By the time I saw the technician
I had fully died had my funeral and been mourned,
my worst fear was that I would have the same number of mourners
turn out that I had
Tupperware party guests.

I had the ultrasound,
the technician told me to check back with my doctor,
because she couldn't tell me anything
until she read the films.

Why doctors have made little game of
don't tell the patient, is beyond me.
I got dressed and walked out of the room,

looking for the front desk.

There was a group of staff
standing in front of this wall of films,
shaking their heads,
even some, "Oh my Gods."
"Excuse me," I interrupted.
"How do I get out of here?"

One of the ladies said,
"This way, I'll show you."
I started to follow her,
I heard someone say,
"That was her, so sad."

I think the lady that showed me to the front heard her too,
she winced and looked over her shoulder to me with a quick smile.

Later that same day,
I received a call from my doctor.
They found masses everywhere.
The uterus was full of masses,
the ovary was covered too.

The other ovary had been removed
several years before with a tumor on it,
when my first son was about two years old.

So, when I had boy - girl twins it was
with one over productive ovary.
That's two eggs at a time!

I had a preop appointment with the surgeon.
He went through a list of things that he needed to
"You're telling me you don't smoke at all?"
"No, I have never smoked"

"Why do you think I am a smoker?"
"The lines around your mouth are classic smoker"

"Oh, I shook my head,
actually, they are classic whistlers lip lines"
I started to whistle.
"I've whistled my whole life,
started when I was really young."

Without a biopsy,
or any kind of test,
the doctor told me they would
do surgery that Friday.

I had three days.
The doctor said they would
remove the uterus,
the ovary,
anything else that was involved.

They would check lymph nodes,
take the appendix, gallbladder,
all that looked suspect.

He looked at me, "You may wake up
to find that you are terminal,
that you will need chemo,
or that it was nothing."

"You should get your affairs in order."
Get your affairs in order?
How does one do that?
I would want my children to know God,
I had done what I felt like I could

The doctor patted me on the shoulder
as he left the exam room.

It was like I was in slow motion.
This just can't be real.

Was I finally going to die?
I think that would be the best outcome.
I could just stop having to deal
with life at all.
A thot.

My husband,
my sisters,
my mother
came to the hospital
while I waited for the surgery to start.

My husband sat on the floor
at the end of the bed.
He was rather,
person non-grata at this point.
We were not getting along
but he felt he should come just in case.

My sisters joked with me,
my mom brought me a gaudy ring
with a huge pink stone in it.
She had no idea about emotion or love.
Who brings a dinner ring to a "loved one's"?
possible
end of life,
party.

They all prayed
then I was taken away.

When I awoke,
I was told I would know sometime the next day
about what the surgeon had found.

Are these people just master torturers?
or what - the next day?

They had done a full
abdominal hysterectomy
found nothing anywhere else.

I was free of that pain-in-the-gut uterus!
Thank you, Jesus!

RECOVERING MYSELF..

The tests all came back
showing no cancer—
the second time anybody had said that word out loud to me.

It took so long to heal up.
I was flat on my back for a total of six weeks
(if you don't count the time
I got up and ended up back at the hospital).

Maybe it wasn't so bad.
After a few weeks in bed,
I started to think that my husband had changed—
that he was changed by this whole ordeal.

Prior to the surgery,
I had gathered several books,
some Christian teaching tapes,
some magazines.

If I took the medicine for the pain,
I had no pain,
but I could not read my Bible
or understand the tapes.

So, with less meds,
I could read,
but the pain was terrible.
I could barely move.
I wanted to be able to know
what was going on in the house,
and know the kids were Ok.

I had moved forward on the divorce,
then been dealt this little surprise.
So, I was all-of-a-sudden sure
that I was unable to take care of myself.

Maybe it would be better now.
I needed to do some studying
and was praying for guidance.
I told myself I better figure out
what chickens eat,
cause I was fully transformed
into a big chicken.

Back at home,
I needed to go to the bathroom,
I called my husband.
He came in and bent over
put his arm out in front of me
to hold on to in order to sit up.

Right then, clear as a bell, I hear,
"Just keep leaning on the arm of flesh."
I was jolted inside,

"Oh Lord, is that you?
I- I am sorry.
Forgive me."
I was going to rely on the man of flesh
who had let me down,
 over and over again.

Why had I not trusted God
to take care of me.
I could always rely of him.

How quickly I reverted back
to a hopeless, helpless soul.
"Lord, as soon as I can walk,
I am leaving this place."

I wonder why that was so clear to me?
God doesn't want divorce

I'm sure –
wishful thinking?
Maybe. I just didn't trust me.
That very afternoon,
I went to the living room—
just to get out of the bed.
It took a lot of assistance
and much pain.

My youngest sons were arguing
over who got to ride the go-cart.
The go-cart that my husband
swore to me would be a shared gift to the boys,
but he had now decided that Sean was too big,
two weeks after it was for both of them.

It was to be for Travis.
He and Sean were arguing.
Sean was very angry because he was sure
of the obvious favoritism
toward Travis once again.

My husband got in front of Sean,
called him a baby,
every other thing he could think of,
trying to get him to fight with him.
He was pointing his finger at Sean's nose
not touching it just close.

He wanted him to throw a punch,
so he could beat him half to death.
I told Sean, "Don't you move."
Sean's nose was flaring,
his stepdad just stepped up the torment.

Sean looked like he was about to get up,
I sprung off the couch and

in between the two of them.
As I had gotten up and lunged,
I felt a terrible pain inside,
as though a huge tear had occurred.

I was instantly crumpled.
"Get me the phone Sean," I said.
He looked mortified. "Mom!"
"Get me the phone--now-- Sean."

He skirted out and brought back the phone.
"Dial Andy's house."
Sean dialed,
I talked to mama Marquez.
"I need for you to come and get Seany
keep him until I tell you to bring him back."
She didn't hesitate.
"I'll be right there."

I told my husband that
I need to go to the hospital."
He stared at me.
"I need you to pick me up.",

"Now!" he jumped and moved to my side.
He bent down and started to lift me,
I screamed. He stopped.
"No matter what I do,
pick me up,
and take me to the car."
He picked me up.

I could not help but scream,
but we went to the hospital
and into the emergency room.
I explained what had happened,
my husband stood there without saying a word.

They didn't say,
"do you feel safe at home?"
"Are your children safe at home?"
They ended up giving me
several injections in my stomach,
told me to take the pain medication,
or I would not get better.

We went home,
I took the knock-me-out medications
until I was able to walk again.

I packed my bags and left that very day.
I was scared and had no idea
if I would ever be able to take care of myself.

This would be the first time
I ever had tried.

GOD'S PLAN TAKES FORM....

I lived in one room where I worked.
They had a vacant apartment
attached to the building
where I worked
for a pest control company.

I took Sean with me
took the twins
when their dad was at work.

He was a fireman
worked three days on
four days off.
It was all I could do.

We did get through the
process of the divorce
and child support.

He was to give me a
percentage of his retirement.
I didn't want to even take that,
but I had to have something
to start this new chapter with.

I was waiting for the check
for a part of the value
of our home.

He wanted the house,
after I walked around the yard
looked at my flowers,
around the house that I had decorated,
I was fine with giving it to him.

I started looking for a place to rent
ended up finding a condo to buy.

My friend who was also a realtor
kept telling me she could find me a condo
for less money than rent.

I really had no thought
that she actually would.
With my equity check,
I would have a good down payment.
I was to meet with him at the title company
 to sign off on our house,
he had to sign off on my new place—
technical reasons of some sort.

He had a paper for me to sign
before he would give me the check.
It was saying that I had
been separated from him
for a couple of years
prior to our divorce.
That would keep me from a
larger share of his retirement.

The title agent could tell
there was some sort of coercion,
what she didn't know was,
it was total blackmail.

If I didn't give them the check today,
I would lose the condo
to a backup offer.
I told her that it was

Ok, I looked him in the eye and said,
"God will make this all come out
just like he wants it to."
I signed his paper.
I decided not to give it anymore thought and I haven't.

I got the condo.
I have no idea how that ever worked out.
I barely had the money to make the payments
needed to work two jobs.

Getting Past the Barriers......

I had all three kids most of the time,
would have kept them all the time,
but their dad wanted them
to be with him half of the time.

Megan was having what I think was a mix
of the divorce and being a preteen.
She was dumbfounded by the divorce
so was Travis.

 All I could say was,
"You don't have to understand"

We had a pool to use and a hot tub.
It was good for the kids to have stuff to do also.
I had always had the house full
of one or more of the boy's friends.

They come over for B&G's.
I loved cooking for them and having a house full.
Now in the condo they still came by
but I had to work 2 jobs,
which made my biscuits & gravy days
somewhat behind me.

I got home one Friday,
the power gate and mailbox area
had yellow crime tape around it.

I figured a delivery truck had tangled
with the awning of the mailboxes.
I pulled into my little garage.
I closed the door and walked inside.

It was cool, and I loved it.
My own place,
drama free I could think

do whatever I pleased, Thank you Lord.

Doorbell right on que.
I looked through the peep hole,
it was my neighbor.
I open the door
She was very serious,
"Did you hear what happened?"
I assumed she was talking about the gate,
"The gate?"
"I sure hope they fix it fast.
She looked shocked,

"You're in trouble for it"

Wait – What? "Me"
why would I be in trouble for it?
"Your son was driving your motor home and hit it",
she looked all kinds of smug.

"I have to go"
I shut the door almost in her face.
I turned around
stood there trying to make any sense of this.
There is no possible scenario
that would have Travis, driving –
let alone driving a motor home.

He was not that kid,
I didn't think anyway.
When someone tells you
they saw it with their own eyes
how do you dispute that?

Just then a tall beer can
on my counter caught my eye.
"The drunk was in my house!"

I can't believe that my house
had that man in it.

I felt like I had been violated.
I called his house, Travis answered.

"Mom, dad showed up at my condo"
"He in his motor home
he misgauged the height & width"

"Oh my God"
"How in the world did this happen?"
"Did you knock the front gate to the complex down?"
"Of course, not mom, he was drunk,
 he plowed right into it."

THE DRIVING PROBLEM...

"The neighbor says
You drove it."
"Mom I backed it out of the gate area,
I was relieved for a part of a second,
I started to take a breath.

Then drove us back to dad's house."
"You drove?
You don't have a license!"
"Mom don't be mad,
I made dad stay in the condo
with a beer while
I got the motor home out of the driveway"

"You left the scene of a crime
you don't have a driver's license!"
"Mom calm down,"

I have a 14-year-old
telling me to calm down,
In what universe?

"Dad gave his insurance
to the neighbor
for the police."
"Wait you left the scene of a crime?
Do you know what that means?"

"I'm coming to get you!"
I was fully crying,
I shouldn't have been driving
there was no way I was leaving them
there one second longer.

Travis was telling me no don't come,
"What do you mean, no?
"Mom, its Friday after 3,

that means we are supposed to be with dad."

"Get your stuff I'm coming to get you"
I had to scream at Megan to get her in the car
Travis was telling me it would be better if they stayed there
to make sure their dad was alright.
"It is not the responsibility of a pair of 14-year olds
to take care of a full grown drunk
who takes his kids' lives for granted"

I got them back to the condo.
Megan stormed up the stairs
slammed the door
got on the phone.

I went to court to try to get
full custody after this occurred,
I took the kids with me.
I was sure they would need
to be asked what they wanted too.

There was surely no way the court
would not see that
this was the only thing to do.
I could not see any scenario
where I wouldn't be walking out
with full custody.

The judge threatened to put me in jail.

He was almost yelling mad at me
for not letting their dad take them
when it was his visitation time,
then yelled at me for bringing the kids with me.
I was in total shock.

"I don't know how this stuff works," I told him,

I assumed you would need to talk to the kids too."
"You are playing on the courts sympathy."

He looked like a mean ogre
holding his gavel like a club.
He was just plain mad.

My thoughts that judges and courts were fair
and would make right decisions was gone.
Poof! Like that gone.

The ogre, I mean judge
told us out to go with our attorneys
to try to make some decisions
on our own
be back in 1 hour.

I was trying to tell him
about the gate
Travis driving,

"Sir, he showed up drunk at my house
had our 14-year-old drive,"
He banged his gavel
said he would hold me in contempt.
He wouldn't listen.

I would almost bet that
he had been in a divorce
custody situation that went against him
himself.

Of course, it wasn't for many years
that I was talking about this stuff
until it made sense.

Turns out the attorneys

either one,
didn't give a flying fig
about him driving drunk,
crashing into my complex,
leaving the scene of a crime
or having a 14-year-old drive.

They split up the visitation
according to my ex's schedule.

He came into mediation
with poster board charts.
He was the master of the chart.
I thought they would laugh him out of there.

He showed when he worked and when I worked
when the kids went to school,
had weekends and vacation.
They both thought it was excellent.

Dumbfounded,
that's the only word for it.

PRAYERFULLY HELPLESS....

He was President and Union negotiator
for Firefighters and Peace officers' Union
of California.

My attorney and His attorney
thought the chart made perfect sense.
No input from me was needed.

"I demand,
that he not be allowed to drink
when he has the kids"
I was literally grasping at straws.
I am not smart enough to figure this out
my kids are going to suffer for it.

He angrily demanded the same of me.
"No problem - I don't drink."

"But I think I will try it
when you have the kids!"
I of course would especially not drink then,
I had no idea when they would call
from a hospital or the police.

He has since lost his job with the State,
although he was not fired
he did get to "retire early".

He says he is scraping by,
is constantly on the wagon,
off the wagon.
He told the kids several times
over the years
if they got good grades
kept the house clean
anything else he thought of,
he would stop drinking.

This time
this alcoholic
has made an unremovable
scar on our family.
His lack of judgement,
recklessness
sickness –
whatever the current beliefs are
have taught me things
I should never have had to learn.

My kids will work their way through
the insidious poison for years
with good and bad results.

The twins were in my constant prayers.
It was almost maddening
to wonder through thoughts of
what might be happening at their dads.

I was praying and begging god to protect them.
I know now they were doing all the things
that my worst worries thought.

I had no way to guide them
or protect them.
It was a particularly horrible
sort of hell.

WHEELS WERE TURNING...

I "got" to keep the van in the settlement.
I also got the very old very
disgusting motor home
that had only been wrecked once.

I had really wanted a small car.
I saw a green Neon and I said out loud,
"Lord, I want a little car like that."
The digital gauges on the Areo Star Van
were all slowly failing.
They would just one by one go blank.

I had put an ad in the paper
to sell the motor home,
it was still at the house.

I had gotten a call,
I sat up a time to meet the guy.
I got the papers together,
just in case the people were interested
in the beat-up piece of junk.

I drove across town and turned down the street
that I had lived on for 11 years plus or minus.
When I stopped at the top of the drive way,
my ex came stumbling up to meet me.

I stopped the car and got out.
He was so ready to help me sell this thing.
"I can show them around in it
and the way things work."
"I want to help you"

I turned around and climbed back to my car.
I was not going to be part of this circus.
I drove to the end of the road
and left down the hill.

I was mad and weepy,

Then the rest of the lights on the dash board went blank.

I had no idea what my speed was or anything else.
I pulled over and put my head on the steering wheel.
Please, Lord help me,
are you there?"

When I was composed I lifted my head
I had parked right in front of the Ford dealership.
"Ahh. Lord?"
"That's you, right?

Please let me be brave and smart.
Don't let me make a bad decision, please.
I started the van up and pulled into the lot.

It only took a second to have some "help" show up.
The salesman did the salesman thing.
I let him look through the van,
I knew what he was doing,
I had sold cars.

Just looking he would run his hand over my paint.
Is there a scratch, without saying a word.
Just enough to shake my confidence.
He wasted that effort,
I had zero confidence.

"I see a lot of work will need to be done on the van"
"Ok, thanks for looking"
I walked around to the driver's side door.
"Oh, wait, I'm sure we could take it in as a trade in".
"You realize that the electrical harness
is going to need to be replaced,
that alone is about $800.00.

He said, "I know,
we'll look at that
when you find your car"
"What are you looking for?"

He started to walk toward some cars.
"I think a small car, used –
would be perfect."
"Ok," He started walking in a different
direction I followed him.,

He first walked up to a tuna boat,
he tried to open the door,
it was locked. Hmm?
Next, he tried another little truck,
it was locked.
"The yard guy must not have brought out the keys"
"I really want something small,
like a Neon"
I had seen a green one,
one day pass me,
it just called my name.
I didn't tell him that.

He said, "Well how about this one?"
I turned around and there was this little
Neon,
Green.

In my head I heard a funny version
of the scary music song on movies.
This was beyond belief.

Of course,
we were on the lot still.
We went in to work the deal.

After working on the payment,
I thought I could afford
he said they would need
an additional $1000 to make the deal.

He asked If I had another vehicle I could trade in.
I laughed,
"I do have an old motor home.
I was going to sell it today,
I even have the title with me"
"Perfect"

I tried to tell him it was a piece of garbage,
he didn't care.
I told him where it was parked,
he said the shop guys would go tow it in.
I must have said
"But" five times.

I was very sure that they would take one look
at that hunk of junk and deal over.
They let me take the car with me to show the kids.

INTEREST PAYS OFF .....

I was going to come back the next day
with proof of insurance and be the new owner.
I stopped by the insurance office
told them the good news.
"Hi Steve,"
He stood up
came to look me in the eye.
"How are you?"

I was so touched by his thoughtfulness
He asked what was up.
"I just had the most amazing morning"
I told him about the prayer
the car and the motor home.
He was very happy for me.

I told him the payment was
a little more than I had hoped for.
"What kind of rate did you get?"
I gave him the paper work.
He looked over it and smiled.

"Ty as your insurance carrier
we can finance the car for you much cheaper."
"I already sat it all up with car lot though"
He started typing something into his computer,

"I can print the check for the payoff amount
you just take it to them"
I got the check,
my payments were twenty-five dollars
a month less too.

I thanked him and hugged him too.
Next stop pick up the kids from school.
I pulled up and I could see them.
They looked and then looked again.

"Mom?"

I got out and put my arms out like Vanna White,
"We got a new car"
"Well new to us new"
"What about the van"
Megan was worried about the van.
"I traded it in"
"Can you afford it mom?"
Travis was trying to be happy
but still responsible or something.

"Don't you worry, I got this"
Me and God, right God.
The next morning, I got my check
and went to the Ford lot.

I took the check to the salesman.
He looked at it for a moment,
"We can't take this"
he got the sourest look on
his previously gleeful face.

"Why can't you take it?
it's the right amount
the right payee,
date, it's all correct"

He said he would have to go talk to his manager.
I followed him down the hall.
His manager ask me to come in to his office.
He wasn't all nice and syrupy this time.
He didn't even stand up.

"The sale is written up with
our finance group that is binding"
I was puzzled

"I still want the car,
I have the full payment right here"
He shook his head no.

"Are you telling me I can't buy the car now?"
He let out a long breathe and said,
"The sale was made so cheaply that the only way
we will make money is with the interest."
Well I guess it was too good to be true.

"Ok then, thanks anyway"
I laid the neon keys on his desk
and turned toward the door.
Before I got one step he said,
"Fine, I'll take the check"
I laid the check down and
picked up the keys.
He was fuming,
I was giddy.

SOMETHING HERE

Lord I just can't believe I could be so,
Grown up!?
Thank you, Father,
for providing more than my needs –
even my wants."

I had to drive pass that car lot at least weekly.
The beat-up piece of junk,
"as represented,"
sat on the lot for 2 years.

It was finally gone one day
They must have demo-ed it.
There was no other explanation
that would make sense.

It was amazing,
I was running my own home,
paying bills,
feeding us
and happy.

I was constantly fearful
that I would mess it all up.
I was afraid to buy anything extra.
I had a car payment, thank you Lord.

I worried so much when the twins
had to go to their dads.
I prayed so much.
I learned way later
that they were off to parties
taking their dads car.

I am so thankful they didn't lose their lives.
This time of my life was handled with prayer.
I wish I could have been more compassionate

to the kids somehow.
The frustration and fear for their lives
was unbearable.
Yet we all survived.

Sometimes survival is just as painful
as not surviving.
I would write a list of my bills
start it with tithes,
on paper there was never enough to pay the bills.

They were always paid.
It was an excellent faith builder.
My doorbell rang one afternoon.
I looked out the peep hole,
it was my mom.
I opened the door

"Hi mom", told her to come in.
Do you want some tea or coffee?
She had walked on into the living room area.

She was looking out the sliding door
that led to my tiny adorable patio.
"I don't like that neighbor so close."
"it's a condo, that's the price you pay,
I don't mind it"

She walked back to the kitchen,
"Ty Beth"
I turned to her.
She was looking at my bill list.
"Ty Beth,
God doesn't need you to pay tithes"

That's for people that have money"

I was surprised but I didn't show it.
"Mom, your right,
God doesn't "need" my money,
He ask that we give some back"

"Remember the widow's mite?"
She was angry.
She turned around and went out the door
without another word.
I decided that I needed to move my
bill list off the fridge.

I was glad that I had taught the kids
that they should give God 10%.
I don't know if they do this,
but they do know God
didn't say it as an option.

A RUNNING BATTLE

The kids are getting older,
they are neither one doing well in school.
It was a fight to get Megan out the door.
One morning I was ready to take them to school
Megan yelled "Come back for me when you drop him off"
I was floored,

'I am making one trip
you go now, or you walk"
She did not come down
I took Travis and dropped him off.

When I pulled back thru the gate
I see their dad's car.
I pulled into my garage
came back out to see what was up.

"Hi Ty, I just came over to take Megan to school"
"Oh well let me just go get all her stuff,
you'll love having her live with you"
His look was panic.

"Whoa what's going on?"
"I told her if she didn't go when I took Travis,
she had to walk."
"If you take her – she's yours."

Megan was pressing past me very mad,
she reached for the door handle and her dad says,
"Megan you're going to have to walk"
Now she was mad.
"I reached back and pulled the condo door shut and locked.
"I'm going for my run"
Her Dad yells, "she can't go by herself"

"She's 16,
it broad daylight,

barely 10 blocks"

"Come on and I'll be with you the whole way"
She was madder than ever.
I stayed about a block ahead of her the whole way.
Her dad went around the block
3 or 4 times looking out for her.

When we got to the light
where she would cross and be at school,
she hugged me and said "I love you Mom"

And that my friends is how a skirmish is won.
The next time the kids were with their dad
they got his permission to take their GED
be out of school.

It didn't matter what I said
they just had to have one parents ok.
I tried to get them to see how important it was
to finish this first big part of life.

I was so sad that they would miss graduation.
"A 16 ½ year old can't even get a job,
I will not leave you sitting here every day
eating and watching TV"

I wanted to cry,
I knew that would not help.
they took the GED
a week later
both passed it.

They can't write high school graduate on applications.
Travis started doing hardwood floors
with a guy who he had helped out here and there for years.
He ended up being good at it.

I kept pushing Megan to get a job.
She went out with one of her girlfriends
looking one day and both got one
at a care home
down the block from the condo.

She said she would never have taken the job
if she knew it required changing diapers
on old people.

She stuck with it
showed me
and maybe herself the depth of compassion
she was capable of.
She would go in and read the bible
to a lady that had been a Sunday school teacher.
She was now too blind to read.
My girl even went in on her day off
to sit with a dying man.
She said he had family right there in town
who didn't even come down.
These are things that make
pockets of strength in a person,
I'm sure of that.

PART 3

ANOTHER YEAR LATER

I was getting ready to go to work
at my second job, at the restaurant.
I stood in the bathroom putting up my hair
I just stopped and looked at myself.

"Lord, I'm lonely"
"Should I think about meeting someone?"
"only if you think so,
don't let anybody wrong get near me –
maybe NEON lights over the head of the right man".
I laughed,
I could hear God laughing too.
Off to work I went,
worrying about the kids when I left
as always,
teenagers home alone…never a good idea.
I came home early on a few occasions
for teenager antics

Work was the hottest restaurant
in the county,
McPhee's Grill

I was ready for a big Saturday night
in great spirits.
Tips were usually hefty on Saturday nights.
Right off two guys
came and sat at either end of the bar,
then seconds later
a guy I knew from church also sat down.
He was a nice guy,
but he just didn't interest me at all.
I greeted each one and filled orders for the wait staff
as they came in.

I was going like crazy.
This handsome striking man came in
sat at the far end of the bar.
For the next few minutes
I was in a whirl!
Each of the men at the bar started to hit on me
one right after the other.
I am laughing in my mind.
"Lord do you have a sense of humor!"
I was spending as little time with each one
as possible
tried to not make eye contact
with the guy from church.
He is so nervous
I know he's about to ask me out.

I got down to the handsome guy at the end,
I was nervous.
He asked me my name,

"Ty" I said.
He put out his hand and said,
"I'm Don"
I took his hand and we shook.
I got him some red wine
he called me by my name,
which was nice and surprising to.

As I went down the bar the church guy stops me
here it comes.
"Ty would you like to go to a movie with me
or something?"
I was just sick,
I didn't want to hurt his feelings or reject him.
"I just don't think I'm ready
to be dating just yet"
I lied,
he was surprised
but ok with it.
He finished his drink and left.

He ended up with another single mom
at church, they made a cute couple.
I check with the first two guys
who flirted with me a little
then made my way back to Don.

He was older than me
but just seemed to be the nicest guy.
He said he hadn't seen me here before
I explained,
"I am only here on the weekend nights"
"my day job",
I made air quotes, "
is for a veterinary hospital
during the week in Atascadero."

He smiled and asked which one,
turns out he was a patient there,
or at least "Bo" was.
Bo was a yellow lab,
she was his love.

I didn't know his last name,
but I figured I could look up
"Bo" with an owner first named "Don".
I was a pretty good detective,
I laughed as I walked down the bar.

I'm trying to cut the two at the other end loose,
it's not working.
I called the host over,

"Could you please seat some single girls
at the bar to help me out."
He laughed, "we've been trying to figure out
what fragrance your wearing,
"ou'da come'n git it"
"Very funny now help me out"
"Two young'ns coming up"

That worked great
they even deicide to go to a table!
I had 6 servers needing drinks,
I got them together as quick as I could.

I had a lull,
I went down to the handsome guy at the end of the bar.
I pull out a tray of glasses and started polishing.
I made sure I paid a lot of attention to the servers,
still gave Don a smile every now and then.
Don asked me if I was single,
was I dating anyone,
would I consider going out with him.

I was again amazed.
I had offered him a second glass wine.
He declined.
I went to print out his ticket
I did something you should never do,
I wrote my number on the bottom.
So- not like me.

I sat the tray on the bar in front of him
still had my hand on it,
he looks up and says,
"Ty can I get your phone number?",
I just looked down and tapped the tray,
he looked down and smiled.

"Oh – well I'll call you!"
He curled his white mustache and raised an eye brow,
very Tom Selleck-esk.
Oh ya he was definitely in the running.
He walked out,
I hoped he would call.

Bo, takes one for the team

435

I was back to work
happy as a clam.
It was vaccine clinic day.
I was busy calling names
escorting people and pets back.

I came to call the next name on the clipboard. "Bo Fox"
I said as I looked around to greet them.
I was stunned,
I looked again at the clipboard,
this time at the owner line.
Owner: Don Fox.

I was so nervous I just stood there.
I realized he was standing right in front of me.
I opened the half door,
Bo was shaking and drooling,
she was scared to death.
"How are you?"
"Don? right."
"Correct" he said.

Bo got on the scale
weighed and got off,
I had to weigh her a second time
because I forgot what it was immediately.

I put Don and Bo into an exam room
hung the chart on the door.
I went to the tech,
"Kim, annual shots in exam 2."

She took one look and me and
followed me to the back.
"What's going on with you?" she was grinning.
"nothing I said" also grinning.

"Do you know this guy?" she wasn't going to stop.
"I met him at my other job the other night"
"Please don't say anything about me to him"
She was really intrigued now,

"You like this guy, don't you?"
We gave Bo her shots about 6 months early.
Kim totally told him I was single,
a great catch
I don't know what all.

MEETING OF THE MINDS

He picked me up for dinner a week later,
in a beautiful silver Porsche.
He treated me very special.
I was so excited with the prospect of this new friend.
I think I skipped over everything that comes before
went straight to, I was in love,
I think I loved him immediately.
He was so different.
He wasn't sweet and cuddly,
but he made me feel like I was special to him
that he respected me
and admired me also.
He told me later that he just saw a short-legged runt
figured he would get lucky.
Me being 5'9" didn't resemble a
short-legged runt in the slightest.

He could be so brash at times.
He took me by his house
under the guise of letting Bo out,
but in fact, it was to show me his house.

We walked into his beautiful house
he held his arms out and spun slowly around,
"is this what you're looking for? – Security"
I was surprised,
without really thinking about it I told him,

"My security & my treasure is in heaven –
if this house and your things
are your security & your treasure
I feel so sad for you –
you will likely be long gone
someone else will have your things"
He stood there looking at me and chuckled,
"So, are you sleeping with anyone?"

Where did that come from?
"No, I'm not.
I'm working hard to be a Christian
I don't sleep with anyone I'm not married to!"
What the heck!

I was having second thoughts,
people continue to surprise me.
"Really." he said this with some skepticism,
"How long have been single?"
"About 5 years",
"Really!" he found this unbelievable.
He let the subject lay.

We looked at the house
the yard
the pool
the sheep
and the boat etc.

When we got ready to go, he ask me,
"Do you mind if I sleep with someone?",
"No not at all –
Just don't bother to call me anymore"..
he again chuckled and said, "understood"

What person in their right mind
would ask these questions
after just meeting a person.
He was a whole different planet
kind of person.

We made weekly drives over to Morro Bay.
We would park the car
walk along the path by the shore,
we loved to eat at the Great American Fish Co.

where we could look at the ocean
even smell the saltiness.
We always brought home a doggie bag for Bo.

I learned that Don was a
jaded public servant of sorts.
He was a retired LAPD detective,
he told most people who asked
that he had been a trash collector for the city.

To say he was jaded with people
and life was an understatement.
He had married his girlfriend
right out of high school
she was pregnant.

It ended badly when he went to Viet Nam.
He signed over his parental rights to her new husband
when she told him that's what his son wanted.
These were his words
I now know only the tip of that story.

HAPPINESS, DULLED.

He later married again more happily,
they struggled to have children.

All sorts of medical intervention were tried,
they finally had a son a beautiful bundle of joy.
A year later they became surprisingly pregnant again.
They had so much joy to have two sons.

It wasn't long after the second son was born
that they became aware that something
was wrong with the first son.

They were stunned
to find out both sons had M.S.
They lived their short lives in wheel chairs
with much pain.
Don took them to the house in Mexico
in the plane
took them hunting,
carrying them in a backpack.

From Don's stories they had exciting
amazing lives.

They died at 12 and 14.
Again, I am only retelling what he told me.
I have no idea what their mom went through
I'm sure it was heartbreaking.
Don had started to attend church with his family
when the boys started school.
The church school was the only place
they could go at the time.

He got to know the pastor
got support in this time.

Before his second son died

Dons, wife had a stroke and went into a coma for a time.
She did eventually come out of the coma and regained her life.
He said she was forever changed,
they could no longer continue the marriage.

He took his son and gave her the paid off house, his words.
Men think a paid off house is a badge of honor,
she owned that house too.
I heard this said by other people.
It made me a bit angry.
It's not my story..

His second son died about a year later.
I asked him, a long time later
what he would change in his life
if he could.

He would have stayed with the boy's mother forever.
I wished I could tell her.

The caregiver who had helped Don
with his son ended up living with him for many years.
He married her when he had a heart attack.
He had to have what he called a "five by-pass".
He had a scar the length of his chest.
When he lay back without his shirt on,
the wires that they used to close his sternum with,
bumped the skin up.

He said he married her because
she stayed with him thru the ordeal.
He later told me he wanted to make sure someone
would not let the doctors pull the plug.

I never was sure if he was the person that he described
himself to be or he was a just covering up a soft heart.

He said he divorced her eleven months later
he had one of his buddies follow her
caught her sleeping with her ex.
She fought it tooth and nail.

When I met Don, he kept from me
that he was still married to her.
He had not finalized the paper work.
He was dragging his feet because
he didn't want to give her any money.

He said he wasn't giving her anything for an 11month marriage.
11 years together previously was something, I told him.

When I found out I told him
I just had to
walk away
he was married.
I thought for a few minutes then said,
"Do you still want to be with her?"
"No, I want her out of my life"
"If you wanted her out of your life
you would just get it over with"

Long story short we took a drive to his attorney in SLO
he signed the papers and wrote the check.
That sure sounded to me like he was interested in me
It made sense to him to get this over with.
Who knows

PAST LAID TO REST

I had planned a trip back to Tennessee,
months before.
I wanted to go see my Grandma Eva.

On the way to the airport
Don ask me if I would be going out?
"I'm going to see my grandmother"
"it's a long story

I will tell it to you if we get to that place"
I got picked up at the airport by my father's brother,
my Uncle Jack and his wife.

Uncle Jack looked like my dad,
It was hard not to stare at him on the ride home.

My aunt Etta Lee said she was making something simple.
Would I mind a fried bologna sandwich
on white bread with a slice of onion
and mustard?

Wow that was a flash from the past.
I loved it.

I called the kids to tell them I made it safely.
They said I was talking with a southern accent already.
I stayed with my uncle for a couple of days.
We drove through town and he said,
the filling station is owned by your 3rd cousin,
your great uncle owns the lumber yard,
another cousin was the first fire chief at our fire department.
He still goes over
sits in front of the station
with the current chief."

We passed a man leading a mule down the road uncle jack waved,
"Lester, he's a cousin too"

"Oh, my goodness are we related to everyone in this town."
He laughed,
"It sure seems like it doesn't it"

I wanted to see Mama Lee's house, we drove out.
I was just about to see the place
that held so many of my best childhood memories.

We pulled up to two little houses
with a vacant lot between them.

"That sure doesn't look like the house I remember
there were no houses that close."

Uncle Jack looked over
"The vacant lot in the middle is where her house was,
it burned down 10 years ago,
they've never built another one."

This was one of the saddest things
I had seen in a long time.
All the farm around the house was gone.
The tree where I got treed by the cows
was nowhere anymore.

We drove back to Uncle Jacks house.
We both went quietly out to the back porch
we sat in big rockers, I just listened to the porch creek.

I love to rock especially on the porch.
I just mulled over the sights of the day.
How sad that Mama Lee's house was gone.

The next morning,
I really wanted to go see my grandma.
I needed to get to the reason for the trip.

Uncle Jack drove me out.
I was sort of nervous for some reason.

Grandma was living in a senior community.
Each house was a little cottage made of brick.
They were perfect little houses all the same
Neat and smart looking.

Jack stayed just a few minutes and headed home.
Uncle Jack was battling lung cancer.
He managed to stop smoking after smoking
for 50 some years.

He went into remission
then it came back two years later
it took his life.

He was a very nice man.
He told me he was sorry
for what us kids had gone through.

I am alright Uncle Jack,
God is good, I hugged him and told him
I loved him.
I'm glad I got back and see Jack
and all sorts of other near and distant family.
They probably still talk about
the way that California girl dressed.

Grandma was still very proper and dressed very nice too.
She said, "I can't believe you would come and see me."
"I have wanted to come for a long time."
I told her with a big smile.

I told her about things that had happened in my life
that were so wonderful.
I told her about my beautiful children

showed her pictures.

"I don't blame you for anything,
my life has worked out to be
a wonderful witness for the Lord.
My testimony is rich and powerful."

I told her I was a kind of Joseph
in the coat of many colors story.
Bad things worked together for good,
and I loved fashion!

"Oh, and I have a sense of humor unrivaled"
"Also, a gift –
I might even go so far as it being
my spiritual gift sometimes"
She laughed and shook her head.

We sat down for a light supper.
I had all sorts of memories coming into my head.

"Grandma, I remember Mama Lees silverware
with those great big handles" Grandma laughed,
"Ty Beth, your holding Mama Lees silverware"
"Oh, my goodness"

It was my hands that were so small.
I was almost disappointed or something.
I was wondering about other bigger than life
things that were in my memories.

Grandma slept on the couch and I slept in her bed.
I started to argue with her,
but I felt I should just do it.

I woke up the next morning and yelled,

"Are you making breakfast yet?
I was hoping for biscuits and gravy"

"I haven't made biscuit and gravy for a long time.
She used canned biscuits, it was a good time.

We walked outside and looked at her flowers.
sat in chairs on her front patio and rocked.
didn't talk much just enjoyed the cool morning.

We went to Cracker Barrel for supper.
I couldn't believe the sides.
Collard greens, hush puppies and black-eyed peas.
I had never been to a Cracker Barrel before,
I was a fan now.

Grandma told me she was amazed
the Strong Christian woman I had become.
"thank you" I said.

I was glad she was pleased.
I told her I forgave her
if she wanted or felt the need for forgiveness'.

"Grandma, God has given me the blessing of forgiveness.
I was the one I had the hardest time forgiving.
The least I could do was share it with you"

"Grandma, I loved this time with you,
I will always remember this time with my Grandma Eva"
She touched my face and said,
"Grandma, just grandma"

I flew home with my new GRITS ball cap.
Girls Raised in the South,
it was as though the trip of this life had come full circle.

I felt more healed and loved and blessed.
Many demons were finally put to rest.
God is Good.

NEW CHALLENGES

Don was full of questions,
did I go out,
did I see any men?

The usual welcome back,
I missed you stuff.

I told him about the need to see my grandma.
I told him the things I needed to say to my grandma.
He said, "You could just forgive her just like that?"
"No, not just like that,
it was 45 years of growing and allowing
God to work in me."
I spent my time with family
ate lots of southern food,
not a drop of alcohol
and loved every minute of it.
Don worked seasonally,
for a boat show company.
He would go to different places and help set up these huge events.
He did some security, but mostly
he just strutted his stuff around.

He got pictures with the Bud girls.
With Cheerleaders,
with Famous people
and with faux famous people too,
like Elvis, or Elvira

I think he loved it.
He had worked with boat show people
for many years they were like family.

I stayed at his house
when he went for the 2 weeks events
I stayed there and took care of Bo.

This time I was watching morning news
I saw the first plane hit the Twin towers.
I was in total panic.

This was unbelievable
was the world about to end?
I got my phone and called Don.

He hadn't seen it yet.
He turned on the TV in his hotel room.
The news was suggesting we seal our windows and doors.
They said water may be poisoned soon too.
He said, "I'm headed home as soon as I pack"
"I love you" I said.
"You too" "stay inside and keep the news on."

The things that occurred that day were like a movie.
The destruction was so big and looked unfixable ever.
I could not fathom it at all.
I called the kids to see if they knew.
They were in shock too.

When Don got home
I broke my vow,
I slept with him

I cried,
he was confused.

I loved him so much
I let myself believe I could casually
just go on like this.
I could not.

I told him I could not do this and not be married.
He, true to himself said,
"You're not that good!"

I let the world circumstances put fear in me.
Look how that turned out.
He said he couldn't afford to start all over again
when I took him to the cleaners.
I protested, "Do I at all seem to be that person?"
He lit up a cigarette and said, "women change".
I was heart-broken.

He poured me a glass of wine and said,
"You don't want to marry me",
I told him with a glare that
he had no idea what I wanted, he laughed.

We continued to banter like
this for months…. and….. months.
I went with him to a wedding
for the daughter of his longtime friend.
We flew down in his plane.
This was so very different
who gets to do this kind of stuff
I loved it.

I didn't have to wonder what this kind of life was like.
It was sweet!
He was always watching me
if I seemed too friendly to someone, he was mad.
I'm surprised that his suspension
did nothing but annoy me slightly.

I know he had nothing to worry about
he would just have to see for himself.
He would randomly ask me
if I would sleep with my ex if he asked me.
I told him so many times,
"I am never ever going to sleep with him ever again."
I was somewhat heated about the constant inquiry –
I said, "I don't ever want you to ask me this again"

He took me out to a nice dinner a few days later.
We were speeding alone in that beautiful Porsche
We had just been seated and received a cocktail.

He looks at me and says,
" you look very sharp tonight"
"Why thank you kind sir"
I smiled and raised my glass.

"And you sir, are the most handsome man in the room"
We ordered dinner
I had taken one bite
he looks at me,

"So are you sure you never
think of sleeping with your ex?".
I was beyond angry,
"No", I tried to dismiss it and move on.

"But what if he came over
was really coming on to you?",
he sat with his hands cupped around his wine glass.
I find that I was so angry I might scream
or even throw something,

I stood up from the booth
opened my purse
tossed two twenties on the table,
"I have told you many times
I'm not interested in anyone but you"

I was snapping my purse and putting on my coat.
He was shushing me and waving me to sit down.

I stormed right by him and for the door.
I called all over trying to get a ride home,
I had given him my last cash and couldn't even call a cab.

I had to swallow my pride
walk over and sit by his car.

When he finally came out, I asked him
 If I could please have a ride home.
He said. "yes, of course."

We got in the Porsche
he tossed the cash back into my lap and said,
"don't you ever do that again"
I didn't even look up I wiped the cash into the floor
"don't worry, I won't"

I noticed that the E brake was on
we were headed up the grade,
"Your e-brake is on" he was totally surprised,
"Thank you", he said in relief.

I went to my car and straight home.
I didn't call him or intend to see him anymore.
It killed me.

BROKEN HEARTS AND COFFEE TABLES...

I talked to God about it every night
ask for strength and guidance.
Why do I want to be with this awful man!

Father can you please help me.
After about 3 weeks I was finally feeling human again.
I talked to my sister before church
she wanted me to go to a yard sale with her after church.

We drove all the way out to
Nacimiento Lake to an old trailer.
The owner was selling everything.

I did like this big coffee table.
Sean and Andy his buddy had broken mine
wrestling in the living room.

They were always such, "Wild asses"
I came home one day,
they were on the couch watching a nature show.
The narrator said, "the wild asses of the Little Rann of Kutch." –

They roared, "Mama, we're wild asses"
they were jumping all around
every time they said.
Wild asses, I said,
"Seany Mitchell, stop saying that"
"Andy Marquez stop!" Andy said,
"We're Wild ass's mama we can't help it"

I laugh until they broke the coffee table –
then we kept laughing.
What kind of mom am I?

Wild asses somehow, has become equal to
Mitchell in many circles.

My cell phone rang and brought me
back from the wild asses.
I answered it without checking to see who it was.
"Hello?" it was quiet,
"Hello?"
I almost hung up figuring the signal
must be lost all the way out here.

"Ty?"
"Yes "
then I realized it was Don.
He said he must have called me by mistake,
"No problem see ya"
I started to hang up.
 he said – "oh are you busy?"

I was irritated now,
"yes"
"So, what are you doing?" he asked lightly.
"Oh, I'm out with some friends",
"oh, where?"
just in town running errands"
"Oh, well,"

-I. Ok,
I hope all's well with you, Bye"
"Oh, you must be busy"

"Don, do you want to talk to me?"
"Why," he asked, "do you want to talk to me?"
 "Ok, Don you called me,
If you want to talk, I'd be happy to stop over later"
otherwise-.
"Sure, he said,
"That would be fine if I'm home"
"No problem another time then, bye"

"Ty?" he sounded a little frantic,
"I'll be home"
"Good, I'll be by in a couple of hours"

I hung up the phone
prayed it was the right thing to do.
It was an hour drive back to town.

It gave my sister time talk some sense into me.
"You have just stopped crying all the time" She was right.
So many things were in the don't column.

I went anyway.
I got there,
he had two twenties
sitting on the counter in the garage.
He had washed the Porsche
found the money in the floor,
he couldn't believe I didn't take it.

"Why did you want to talk to me?
"I wanted you to take the money back"
"I'm not a hooker, Don"
"whoa, nobody called you a hooker"
"You did the next best thing"

He picked up his cigarette and
put the ash tray on the other side of him,
so the smoke wasn't in my face.

"Ty, you don't want to marry me?'
he sauntered over to his stool in the garage
and sat down with his cigarette.

"I told you Don, don't tell me what I want –
you obviously don't know"
 "Can we just start again? he asked

with his hands planted on the counter.

"No, we can't start again"
I stood up and the tears began to fall,
I was getting my senses back and was going to leave.
"Oh, don't start that" he said –
"I'm not starting anything
I'm mad and hurt and a woman and we cry –
get over it"

"I have invested my heart and soul into this relationship.
I gave myself to you feeling that you loved me
wanted me"
he came over and wiped my face with a paper towel
"you look so ugly when you cry".
"that's ok, you look ugly when I cry too"

"If that is all I'll head home."
He wanted me,
but he wanted me on his terms
no marriage.

I told him we should just let this time be over for us.
He didn't want that either.
Stale Mate.

He called to see if he could take me to lunch
or dinner
or for a ride to Morro Bay.
I would go
then have him bring me home.
I thanked him for the nice time and went inside.

I had started working for a Veterinarian Clinic in Cambria.
The doctor had owed the Vet hospital I worked at in Atascadero.
I had worked for him there for a good 13 years or more.
He was happy to have me come to work for him in the new place.

I became the manager
learned to be an OJT Vet tech of a sort.

I felt such relief being there it was like I was home again.
Dr. O was always and still is the nicest man in the world.
The things he put up with
probably put him in line for sainthood.

Don and I went out fishing in his boat out of Morro Bay.
We caught maybe 10-15 what he called Football Tuna.
They were about two feet long, maybe longer,
shaped like a football.

We went back to his house
We we're working on the cleaning part.
I had all these cleaned canning jars out on a towel
he would chop chunks
I would stuff them in the jars.

We didn't add anything to the jar but fish.
That was the best tuna ever.
We were just about done,

Sean pulled up out front.
It was Fourth of July,
"Seany" how are you son?"
I hugged him.

He was overcome with emotion to the point of tears.
"Sean what is it?"
"Andy's dead"

My mind whirled he could never have said what I heard.
"What? How? What happened?"
"He was driving a truck for the trash company
his bumper had caught
a warning sign that was too far out in the road"

464

He was sobbing.

"He hit a tree and was killed immediately"
"Oh, my goodness, this could not be true"
I thought of Mama & Papa Marquez,
we had worked so hard to get those boys to
buckle down at graduate from high school.

He was barely out of high school.
Sean & Andy & Jared were inseparable.
I ask Sean if he wanted to stay for a while,
he was going to the Marquez's.
I think he had asked me to go also.
I was in such shock, I said, no.
I wish it were possible to go back.

Dealing with death is one of the most horrible things in life.
The boys had all been trying to be good role models
for each other and Andy was the ring leader.
I don't think I was a good friend that day.

Andy's funeral, "Celebration of Life"
was later that week.

Sean and Jared spoke together,
they literally held each other up.
They committed to continue to follow the path
that Andy had set them on.

I think they maybe had a couple bumps,
but Jared has become an amazing man,
husband, and father, who is also a pastor.

Sean went into Air Force,
Special Ops and was deployed many times.
He received many awards and

commendations for heroic acts.

He has been forever changed by this.
Jared has come to Sean's aid
on multiple occasions and officiated at his wedding.

Sean is a very strong man
he has so much faith.
He said he had no fear when he was in battles,
because he wasn't going one minute before
God called him home.

My fear however, was multiplied.
To see that one of these dear sons
could be gone in an instant was terrifying.

I had two sons in the military
that I prayed continually for
wrote letters to night and day.
Nick and Sean both reached out to me for encouragement
for proof that what they were doing was right with God.

I told them Jesus has said
whatever you do as a soldier do it to the
best of your ability to follow orders,
not be cruel,
be content with your wages.

God knew we would have wars
that we would have to have our young men fight them.
I treasure the letters that I received from them.
To read in print the suffering and pain they went through
the almost inability to survive some things,
both broke and swelled my heart for them.

On the other side more than 15 years later,
it gives me pause to see the fortitude

that has produced their families,
their strength and their trust in God.

Everybody at work would ask for
updates on where the boys were
If I had heard from them recently.

I would start to freak out ever so slightly
if 2 weeks went by and
I haven't heard anything.

I was working in Cambria,
Dr. O again was my boss,
all was right with the world.

It was now when Don called to take me to lunch.
Dr. O said, "Fine take as long as you like
as long as it's no more than an hour"
"Thank you, sir," I said.

I was watching out the window
trying to be inconspicuous.
When Don pulled up in front in his truck
I felt giddy,
what a goof I am.

It was a nice treat
I was happy as a clam to see him.
We drove over to Moonstone beach
parked to watch the surf.

I love the sight and the noise
the salty air of the beach.
I was just sitting there enjoying it all.

He reached over opened the console
and pulled out a little box.

I did a double take; my mind was blank.
He opened the box and showed me
this beautiful diamond ring.
The ring, I thought I would never see
here it was.
He looked at me and said,

"Ty will you marry me?"
I just started screaming
jumping up and down,
he looked at me real serious,
"Ty – you didn't say yes"

YES YES YES, I cried, it was so wonderful
I was to the moon.
I was half over the console hugging him.
He was laughing.

He even got a setting with
the diamonds channel set so that I could
wear my surgery gloves and not snag them.
I couldn't wait to be Mrs. Fox.

STILL THE RING, OF WEDDING BELLS...

It took another year before I was ready to leave
because he wouldn't set a date.

We once again had gone to the house in Mexico.
He told me we would get married in Mexico.
It was Thanksgiving.
We have a good time with friends.
I was afraid to say anything
I didn't want to hear the wrong answer.
We headed back home,

I had thought he was going to go to someplace
in one of the small towns
we would get married.
I reworked the scenario over
and over to get to the wedding part.

The closer we got to home to more resigned
I was that this would finally be the end for us.
When we got home to his house
I got my purse and told him I was headed home.
He said, "Not yet we have the Shrimp to clean and eat"
"You have not been right since we left Mexico"
"What's wrong?"
I looked at him, "you said we would get married in Mexico"
he dropped his head

"The minute we crossed the border home I knew it was over"
"Ty what do you want me to do?"
"Marry me" I said,
"Today"
"Today?"
 How can we do that?
"Today or its finished"
"Ok tell me how"

I could not believe he was saying these words.

I had been on the end of a line like this too many times.
"You go get the license and I will look for a chapel.

He got in my car
went to the county office
came back with the license.

We found a bookstore/Chapel in Morro Bay.
Right across from this coffee shop called Two Dogs.
We got married we both cried.

The pictures were beautiful they took my breathe away.
When we walked out, he said, "Mrs. Fox,
what would you like to do now?"

We both looked across the street, there was a
Two Dogs coffee.
Off we went
bought a pound of Two Dogs,
"neutered"

Dog was what Don and Phil, his best buddy.
called each other.
We sent the coffee to Phil and his wife
by way of wedding announcement.

We were married.
I could move to his house
and stay with him forever.
Exhale.

The day was, Dec. 3, 2002.
Mr. & Mrs. Fox, finally.

We had the best life ever,
we would fly the plane to Mexico

land on the beach
stay at the beach house for a week at a time
go out fishing on the boat in Morro Bay and trips to Cabo.

We enjoyed each other so much,
when he finally decided.
I was not going to take his stuff!

He was diagnosed with lung cancer Jan,12, 2003
gone a week before that next Thanksgiving.

I know I skipped a lot,
I would have so many memories over that last 11 months.
Don was never one to say,
"I Love You"
he even told me once when I had prompted
him to say those three little words,
"I told you I love you,
if that changes I'll let you know"
I turned it around on him our first married,
well our only married Christmas.
I told him I wanted those
three little words for Christmas,

He said, "I Love You?",
"NO silly, Solid Gold Bracelet"
"I knew it!"
He smacked himself on the forehead.
It was pretty funny we both laughed.

We had sold the plane right after the initial diagnoses
"Bo" his sweet yellow lab,
His other blonde,
had been limping for a while.

I took her to work with me

x-rayed her back legs,
she had bone cancer in both back legs.

I held her on my lap
held Dons hand
when we put her down in March of that last year.

I worked for Dr. O off and on for 18 years.
I would never go back,
it was just too painful.

I prayed constantly that God would heal him,
I had people tell me he would be healed.
I now know better than to tell someone the mind of God.

But I grabbed hold of that possibility
even when the doctor told us
there was nothing else he could do.

Don grew so much during the year of suffering.
He told me one day that he was afraid to die
because he had sold his soul to the devil –
begging him to save his sons.

I was so happy to be able to lift
that awful burden for him.

"Don, you're not going to hell,
you can't sell something you don't own,
the devil can't buy something that
Christ paid for with His life"

Don just sat there with his mouth open,
"How did I ever get you?"
"Just blessed I guess"

I told him that the devil

did not and could not keep his end of the bargain,
because his native tongue is the lie
he can't speak anything but lies
with the occasional 1/2 truth
which is still a lie.

He knows his fate
and is trying to take as many with him as possible,
but you will not be one my love.
My husband was teary eyed,
"Will we still be married in Heaven?"
 my heart just swelled and broke,
what a struggle it has been to finally get to be his wife.

"Honey, the bible says that death dissolves marriage,
but you won't care a bit.
You will be with your sons
they will be whole and will have been so,
longer than they suffered on this earth."

He pulled me into his arms which I loved.
I cried and praised God.

We decided to take a road trip.
Don drove the Porsche all the way to Huntington beach.
He slid that silver beauty into the Balboa Beach Club
The valet came around and opened my door
Put out his hand to asset me from the car.

Meanwhile that gave Don the opportunity to
get out get himself out without attention.
He still had his strut,
he put one hand on the small of my.
This will always be a thrill to me
every time I think of it.

We checked into a beautiful suite.

We sat out on the patio and watched locals boating.
Room service knocked at the door, bearing two martinis.

One with three olives just like I like mine.
How did they know?
Don took a shower and dressed for dinner
I was ready soon after that.
Down the stairs into a beautiful dining room we went.

We saw a poster announcing an Oldies Band.
We both smiled at that.

Dinner was two Filets and salad.
We both just picked at it some.

When we heard the music start,
He stood up and held out his hand,
Mrs. Fox may I have this dance?

Are you sure?
I was concerned for his feet.
I am fine, let's dance.

We went to the floor
No one was there but us.
The music was slow but had a sway to it.
He held me close with our
hands entertained between us.

I have no idea what the song was.
I have no idea if others were dancing.
I can see his eyes filled with love.

When he spoke, it was sweetest
deep tones.
Have I told you how proud I am
that you're my wife?

I know I blushed.
You are the most beautiful woman in the room.

He held me close
The song ended,
but the bubble wasn't popped

We made our way back to our room.
He was exhausted
I helped him with his shoes,
over his complaint of course.

Two days later we were headed home.
When we got to the car,
The valet had the door open
Don bowed slightly and said,
Mrs. Fox how about you drive home.
Me? OMG!
He went around to the passenger side
Got himself in and buckled up.

Try not to kill me, he said
There, he's back,
my wise cracking, stinker.
My amazing husband.

I'll try not to, I laughed

It was a long drive back
He slept most of the way.
Porsches aren't known for sleeping comfort.
he was exhausted
He had done this for me.

FADE TO SEA TURTLES AND DOLPHINS...

He had undergone many rounds of chemo
the cancer had spread to his liver,
game over.

The liver filters out stuff like chemo drugs.
He seemed very weak
suffered from neuropathy in his hands
and up to his knees,
that is a numbness
nonstop tingling
like when your foot falls asleep.

He was uncomfortable being touched
he said walking felt like balancing on rubber balls,
like the bottom of his feet were rounded and numb.
The chemo was so awful I don't know how he stood it.

Day, one was alright, day two a little worse,
the rest of the week was horrible.
Then a break
start all over for months.

He didn't want me to sit with him during chemo,
half the time he would drive himself
without telling me he was leaving.

You couldn't tell that man anything.
About 10 months in I got a call from Hospice.
They wanted to come by and talk to me.

I was so worried about leaving Don alone,
I put a baby monitor next to the bed.
I was talking to the woman from Hospice in the kitchen,
when he came around the corner
carrying the baby monitor.
"Why are you spying on me?"
"I wasn't spying on you,

I just wanted to be able to hear you if you called me."

"Why can't I hear you?"
"We don't have to have the monitor
if you don't want it."

He plopped it down on the table
went into the living room.
I told the lady that this
would be a good time to talk to him.

She looked at me and said,
I'm not here to help your husband
I'm here to help you.

She was going to help me get through the process.
What process?
She explained that Don would
soon not have food or drink at all.
"Wait?"
"Are you saying not to feed him?"
She said, he would not eat or drink from here on
because he doesn't want to.
I was very shaken up by this.
I don't think I need you to help me.
She said she would check back with me in the morning.

Don got up to go to the bathroom
after the Hospice woman left.

I was trying to help him down the hallway,
but he slapped at my hand
slammed the bathroom door in my face.

The doctor told me to apply 1
½ morphine patches
instead of just one now.

I was concerned that he would fall or something.

I stood outside the door not knowing what to do.
Megan walked into the back door about that time.
"Where's Don?"
"He's in the bathroom."
"How long has he been in there?"
"About 5 minutes now"
"Mom go in and get him."
"I don't want to embarrass him"

Megan went out the back door and around
to the bathroom window.
She came back in
"He's standing at the sink,
just go in and get him."

I opened the door with the pass key.
He was standing holding on to the counter,
his pants were around his ankles.

I grabbed his pants and pulled them up.
He looked at me and said, "I'm Superman"
I said, "Yes you are"

I told him Megan was there and
wanted to see him.
"Megan's here"
he let her guide him back to the couch.

They talked a bit and she cried.
"He said Megan, don't you cry"
she said, "I love you."
He said, "I love you too"
I got my camera and took their picture.

I thought it would be something Megan would treasure.

I had not realized what he looked like.
Through this slow progression.
The pictures were beyond shocking.
I still have them, for some reason
I can't throw them away.

Days later he was slipping away
he got lost in another place,
he thought he saw dolphins jumping
sea turtles swimming by.
I would just say wow, how neat.

LOVES LIGHT SHINES

482

He couldn't get up and down for a couple of days,
he slept on the couch
I in the floor in front of him
listening for his every move.

The third day he wanted to go sleep upstairs.
I held on to the back of his pants
to get him safely up the stairs
with him swatting at me the whole way,
"I can do it!"

He had not eaten or drank for more than a week,
this worried me.
I was so exhausted
afraid to sleep that he might wake up
and try to go down the stairs,

I closed our door and put a chair in front of it.
I laid in bed well over on my side
prayed that God would stop his suffering,
I wanted so bad to have him hold me
in his arms and say I love you,
I silently cried.

He got up and walked to the bathroom.
He was very lucid.
When he came back
he drew me tightly up to him,
"Have I told you how much I love you?",
I was crying and smiling and praising God.

He got up a second time
and again, went to the bathroom
when he returned, he drew me up again tightly in his arms,
"have I told you you're the most beautiful woman in the world?"
I was again smiling crying and praising God.

He got up one more time
when he came back, he looked me in the face
kissed my eyes, nose, and mouth and said,
"have I told you I'm the luckiest man in the world?"
this time I giggled like a school girl and cried.

Three times Lord, that's all you.
You answered my prayers 3 times over.
At some point in the night
I thought he wet himself,
I tried to change his pajamas.
He started slapping at my hands
"no momma" he said, over and over.

He was covered with black liquid,
I couldn't get him dressed or all the way back on the bed.
"Please lord don't let him remember this"
Don did not wake up the next morning.

I called the Dr. and he helped me get him changed and back into
bed.
He told me he wanted to have a hospital bed delivered downstairs.
I said ok.

Then he said,
"I think you should wait until after Thanksgiving
to have the funeral."

What?

My husband is still alive,
what are you saying?

Why would he say this to me?
He seemed detached, he was our friend.

We had bible studies together

went to the same church.
It was as if he didn't know me.

Travis who adored and loved Don as a second dad,
carried him down the stairs
with one of his buddies.
Don looked up at Travis and said,
"don't drop me asshole",
Travis laughed and said I won't you old derelict."

This sounds terrible,
but it was always their banter,
one last time.

WAS HE REALLY GOING...

They put Don carefully in the hospital bed,
Travis kissed him on the forehead and ran from the house.

He didn't open his eyes anymore after that,
he was barely breathing
he had morphine patches on his back
he just slowly left over the course of that day.

I was so tired
I tried to stay awake
It was like I guilt ridden
I wanted to sleep and at the same time
was horrified that I could even think of me.

My family was there,
I had been up for 3 days watching over him
I told my sister I just need to close my eyes,

when she woke me up –
I was jolted, "oh no, was I asleep?"
I've missed time with him, no no no.
I did not want this to happen.

I got off the couch, "Is he ok?",
my sister was at my side,
"He is almost gone."
I just stood there

"Ty tell him you love him",
my sister pressed me forward,
I gently kissed his forehead
I love you,
tell the boys hi from me"
his breath came out one last time
he was gone.

Now what?

My world was over,
just like that?

Here lay the man I adored
loved so much it hurt.
He would never have a glass of his beloved red wine again
or curl that sexy mustache around his finger again.
I saw his smile

How often he surprised me with the skills he had.
His life knowledge and mostly,
his silly hat backwards whistling dance.

I heard my sister telling me I needed to call someone,
I will in a minute.
"Ty it's been 3 hours", .
Oh.

I called the doctor
he would record the time.
I called the Neptune society to come pick him up.
He had made those arrangements
years earlier.

It was about 3 am when they arrived.
Mike said, "mom lets go in the den
while they get him ready to go".

I walked with him like a sleep walker.
I think we talked about something,
but I don't know what it was.

I heard a noise and looked up,
there was a gurney with a black bag on it –
I broke down totally,
"oh no, oh no, I didn't want to see him in a bag."

Mike held on to me and they left.
Andrea came in to calm me down,
"sissy I watched them,
they treated him with respect."

"He is not in that body anymore"
I couldn't get myself to calm down
I thought I was going crazy.

 I remember my sister Faith sat on my bed with me
 I begged her to stay until I feel asleep.
The doctor had given me, something to take and I took it,
they pretty much all insisted that I take it.

There was much more to this story,
It was so hard.
I cried the day they told us the chemo wasn't helping
I begged Don on my knees not to die not to leave me.
He told me I was not to cry again.

I had to go back a week or more
before he died and tell him
I would be ok, that he was free-
he didn't have to stay here for me.
He looked at me and was confused,

"Am I going to die?".
"Yes, my love, we all will someday",
looking back,
it, all went very fast after that.

There was Thanksgiving
a funeral and so many tears,
I at last could cry and cry I did.
The doctor put me on some kind of medication
after the funeral that just made me blank.
I just didn't feel, for another month or two

No good deed goes unpunished,

490

In January I got a registered letter from an attorney.
Don's son from his childhood was suing me.
I had met him a couple of times

Don had told me not to contact him
or tell him he was sick
or that he had died.

He left his son a 25-thousand-dollar insurance policy
I had wanted him to know his dad loved him,
I called in December
when I received the first Christmas card in a couple years.

I had just sold my condo
put the money in the bank
2 weeks before Don died.
There had been a bad earthquake that year.
The pool was cracked pretty bad.
Don got the pool company out
had the whole thing redone.
He walked around that pool every day,
his pain with every step
was only visible in his clenched jaw.

He made sure it was done right.
When that was finished
he finally decided he was ready
to lay down.

He had said, "I'm not ready to lay down yet"
So many times, before we ever knew he had cancer.
It was his way of saying he wasn't ready to die.

He was ready to lay down.

I was now working two jobs again
to pay the bills on the house.

Don's retirement died with him.

We sold the Porsche before he got real sick
the guy who bought it said he would come get it
after Don was gone.
He did.

That money went to the bank.
The court decided
I couldn't use any of the money
or sell anything especially the house.

It was a terrible ordeal which lasted almost 18 months,
cost $67 thousand dollars in court and attorney fees,
but didn't break me.

Don's son got nothing and wasted his inheritance too.
I could not believe that the world
could allow such a thing to happen.

He had attempted to prove I had killed his father
plotted with his best friend and PD motor partner
to steal all his money and belongings.

The judge sat with his head down most of the time
with his jaw clenching and unclenching.
When the opposing attorney suggested
that I had overdosed my husband with morphine,
I thought I was going to prison.

The judge jumped to his feet and said,"
Are you saying that Mrs. Fox killed her husband?"
The opposing attorney said,
"We hope to prove that, yes"
The judge spat,
"Too my chambers NOW!"

I sat there sure that I was going to prison.
Every time I had stood before a judge in my life it went badly.
When the attorneys came back into the courtroom
my attorney looked smug.
I was confused.

I tried to ask her what was happening.
She held up her finger to stop me as the judge said,
"This poor woman has suffered enough,
there will be no more mention of anything to do with her killing her husband,
do I make myself clear?"
"Yes, your honor"
came the response from both attorneys in unison.

The opposing attorney produced birthday cards and
Christmas cards that he said
were sent to the grandkids from their granddad
proving that Don would not have cut the son out of his will.

I was handed the cards
I looked them over.
The judge asks me if I had ever seen the cards before.
"Yes" I said.

"When did you see them Mrs. Fox?"
"I bought them,
wrote in them
added some money,
then mailed them."

The son was mad he said,
"This is my dad's handwriting!"

The judge asks me if it was Don's handwriting.
"No, it is not his handwriting"

"Each card is signed 'Love Grandpa Fox' –
My husband never signed love,
and he would never call himself Grandpa.
"I wrote them all."

"I have a card he did sign,
if you would like to see it?"
The card was a silly birthday card
he had picked out for me.
There was no love signed to it.

The judge laughed at the silliness of the card.
He said, I believe it is clear that
the handwriting on the children's cards
was not Mr. Fox's
but Mrs. Fox's.

The son said I would not let him
talk to his father when he called.

The judge asks him how many times he had called.
"I didn't call, he said
"I knew she wouldn't let me talk to him."

Even I sat there with my mouth hanging open.
I felt sorry for this man
being egged on by what had to be
the worst ambulance chaser ever.

The judge asked me if had ever
kept the son from talking to his father.
I almost laughed but I didn't.

I know I was supposed to only answer the question asked but I said,
"No one told my husband what to do ever"
"The thought of me controlling him
or his activities is almost humorous."

My dear young attorney was such a wonderful woman,
strong and so amazing.
Her husband had been badly injured
suffered a traumatic brain injury
due to a bicycle vs car accident
one week prior to this case starting.

I was praying for her and her family
and trying to be supportive.
I decided that if I was able to think about her
be prayer support for her
it would help us both.

After the family doctor
the oncologist
friends
even our attorney friend who wrote our wills all testified,

I was questioned as to the where abouts of the
Porsche,
Truck,
Plane,
house in Mexico,
house in Atascadero,
and even the dog –
it finally ended.

They just ran out of questions

It was settled with prejudice or without I don't know –
It just meant they could never sue me, again.
It just ended.

Don's son was not going to be in my thought anymore.
I would pray one last time that he could see how lost he was
that he was in charge of that.
He needed to turn his eyes to God.

People make choices many times a day.
Sometimes they don't choose.

Spoiler alert – that is still a choice.
Mind blowing really.
We cannot just wander about the earth
stumble here and there
and think we are victims
of other people's choices!

When something is introduced into your space
you make a choice –
Woe with me perhaps, or
I don't think so!
We are always "1" choice away
from being on the right track.

If the wrong choice has been made,
back up, change course and start over.
Even if there is a "do over" every 30 minutes
for the first couple hours of your day.

Be actively choosing all the time –
don't let your auto pilot engage.
Turns out
 "Auto" is a bad pilot!

LIMBO FOR NOW

I spent time at home just being there.
I was so lost and didn't have any motivation.
A dear friend from church came to see me
said they were looking for someone where she worked.
I started to work for a large Cardiologist office in SLO.
I went into the job cold no experience
with human medical at all.

 Well, if you don't count my 20+ years as Dr. Mom.
Of course, I wasn't expected to be a doctor.
That was a good thing for,
I was fairly lost and
made multiple mistakes.

I probably shouldn't have started working yet.

I paid the final payment to the attorney
hugged her goodbye
It was like losing a friend.

I had a whole group of new friends,
that I didn't know yet.
My Virgie was a stinker she "acted"
like she was kind of mean and unhelpful
most folks just left her alone.
She was my first project.

Virg and I are still buddies many years later.
We became Grandma's about the same time
which we both found to be the best thing in the world.
We shared similar events to our first grandchild.
They were babies when our sons
had married their moms.
We were both over the moon.

I was at the Cardiologist office
for about a year when one of my co-workers

ask me if I wanted to go to a Botox party
at the plastic surgeon's office down stairs.

I guess I was in an odd mood, go figure for me.
We went,
they would not take her check,
which was par for the course
for this little lady.

She gets me to pay her 200 dollars
in exchange for her being my
personal trainer for 3 months –
Deal!
She was a great trainer
I got every penny worth.

While waiting for the doctor
I scanned some pamphlets
about a tummy tuck.
I had talked to Don wanting to get this done,
he said if I did it - I'd probably leave him
for someone younger.

I was crying softly when the doctor came in.
He asked if I was afraid,
"No", I told him,
Happy! -and I handed him the pamphlet
I want one of these!

I made an appointment
for a month later and
got the surgery.

I was going to Hawaii with my girlfriend
we scheduled the trip for the first day after
the doctor said I would be able to go.
I had shopped for a bikini and everything,

Nice huh? –

Not so fast.
When I got home from the surgery
my daughter was taking care of me,
she noticed right away
that the center of my abdomen
was turning purple
she called the doctor
he said watch it
come back in tomorrow,

by that time
I had the beginnings of Gangrene.

I don't know any other word
that would throw this much fear in a person. –
the area slowly died and sluffed away.
I had a huge hole in my lower abdomen
that was just open,
a perfect circle.

I went to Hawaii with my friend.
I had bandages and
burn cream for the area
that had to be cleaned and changed
twice a day.

When we got home, I started on a bedsore machine,
it is a suction devise that is taped over the area
and carried around 24/7.

It took about 6 weeks for the machine
to clean out all the dead stuff
then I was left with a "cup holder" looking spot.

I told the doctor I wanted it fixed –

we chatted back and forth for a while
I told him I had no intention of suing
but at the same time, I knew he of all people
would be most motivated
to fix-it!

He did a skin graft from my upper thigh –
note to self- avoid skin grafts at all cost.
Most painful thing ever.
The end result,
was a more attractive
"cup holder" –

when I again voiced my disdain
he actually stood there and said,
"You are still the most beautiful naked woman, in the room" –
"No one will even notice it" –

I took a slow breath in and refused
to give in to the urge to scream at him.
I calmly said, "
#1 I am a recent widow –
#2 I have no intention of anyone seeing this –
and #3
It bothers "ME"
that is what is important."

He apologized,

While at the same time making it clear
that this was not at all his fault.
He said he would be unwilling
to do anything further
for at least a year.

I booked a trip to Europe

I stayed for 6 weeks,
I decided that before anything or anybody
took anything else from me
I was going to get away.

In the end the doctor declined to do anything further
as "my body" was probably going to do this again.
Two words: Geezalou!

He was a nice man and truly honorable,
he was killed in an airplane
crash 5 years later,
on his way with a group of doctors to do some
"Doctors without borders" work with children
in some 3rd world country.

I'm healed up and recharged.
I was ready for Europe.
I would spend some money on me.

I loved Germany,
France,
Chezk,
the food was amazing
scenery was breath taking everywhere I looked.

I was admired by many
that felt wonderful.

Truth be told my 'cup holder"
was like wearing your granny panties 24/7 -joke!
Just kidding.
Well, mostly kidding.

I had the experience of walking around in the louvre.
I walked down streets in Paris.

I saw buildings coated with gold leaf,
The Palace of Versailles was breath taking.

There were portions
of the first renderings of the
Statue of Liberty,
the giant torch on a street corner
with gold covering it.
I couldn't understand how people
just walked past
these things
didn't even seem to notice.

Fests in Germany were like
old fashioned fairs
in the states
but with huge steins of beer.

I quickly learned the raising one finger,
your pointer meant 2.

If you only want one giant stein of beer
you raise your thumb,
which means 1.

I went to a concentrations camp
where untold number of Jews were slaughtered.
There was an enormous dome of
dirt in the middle of the camp.

It turned out to be the ashes

Ashes of those burned in the ovens.
This place was cold and foreboding.
There was not much conversation
just time spent trying to fathom
the evilness that had thought this horrible place up.

From there my son and I climbed up a small mountain,
by Colorado standards.
The top had the remnants of a castle.

I saw Karlovy Vary the sister city of Carlsbad in the states.
The smell wasn't appealing
but the scenery almost made me not smell it,
almost.

I visited many churches.
They all had giant statues of Mary holding a tiny Jesus.
It made me sad to think people put
Mary before our Savior.
The proportions made her
so much more important.
When it was time to take
that 20 some hour flight home

I was ready.
I was for the first time in my life
just doing whatever I wanted.
I loved every minute.

The movie on the flight home was,
Last Holiday, with Queen Latifah.
Filmed at the famous
Grand Hotel Pupp,

I had just been there, in Karlovy Vary.
How amazing that was.

Alas, home again. – the real world.
That is when God sent me help,

in the form of my very best friends in the world.
The two K's their first names both start with K,
just the most wonderful people in the world.

Probably our only point of contention was Lib vs Cons.
So, I just try to keep my conservative ideas to myself
let my Godly side be my guide.

We are like family
it really happened so naturally,
they needed a place
(they sold their house and were having one built in AZ.)
I needed the company
the help too.

The house and the yard are just too much for me.
It was so good for me to see how other people think
and act and feel about all kinds of things.

They moved in while I was at work.
When I got home the pantry
had lost its echo and the fridge too.

Kerry said, "Who has 12 containers of yogurt in their fridge
and nothing else?"
I raised my hand.
Don't forget the lightbulb.

"So, do I get to eat some of this stuff?" She laughed.
"TB, what will we do with you?"
"Rhetorical?", I said. Ken and Kerry both busted up.

TOO OLD TO NOT KNOW ME YET

I was in a place,
I could be whoever I am..
many times, in my life I have been
"the runaway bride"
one of my favorite movies,
kind of just fun and silly.
But it spoke loudly to me.

The "bride" had run away
from several weddings,
but the thing that got me
when the reporter was interviewing
her ex's
they all said
she liked her eggs like they did.
Fried,
scrambled,
boiled.

That was me..
I didn't know what I liked-

I liked making people happy.
My thoughts and feelings weren't important.
That silly film helped me so much.

I started trying to see if "I" knew
what I liked.
Sounds crazy –
I had to decided ..
so, I just tried everything.
I try to speak my mind.
I think that will always be difficult for me.

It is so freeing.
I'm still kind and tactful.
I feel like my opinions are relevant

and valuable
sometimes
I voice them.

Don has been gone about 3 years now
I started to think about how I missed
someone to share my life with.

Tons of guilt fell on me to the point
I couldn't hardly function.

I went and talked to my godly councilors…
women I had been in bible studies with
for 10 years or more.

They would tell me what was right
not what I wanted to hear.
I was in shock when they all said,
"Date"
your young and obviously need to share your life
with someone else –
that is what Don would want"

Well that was not expected.
I really had thought they would
council me to stay single
and go into the mission field.

That might have been a relief.

But… go back out there
see if I was a grown up yet…
that was very frightening indeed.

Everything changed,
my new friends were now my most beloved family.
It was so good to have them there

to learn to just live slow and easy.
I decided to get online to a singles site.

They laughed at first,
but they were also supportive if not curious.
They looked forward to every coffee date I had.
I had no idea there were so many,
dare I say 'wackos" out there.

It was good practice
safe with coffee dates to.
I did learn I was still very vulnerable.

I wanted to answer questions
the way I thought they wanted to hear.
I tried to be more interested in them.

I wasn't looking for someone interested in me.
I guess I have to grow and change
just keep trying
learn to be assertive.

It made me somewhat disappointed
that I still needed to be liked more
then I needed to like.

It is so hard,
I decided that the way to do it
was to plan it in advance.
To plan answers
plan reactions,
plan, escape routes too.

Do not give out my address
phone number
or very much information about myself,
plan to see if I liked them

not if they liked me.

I had to think through
scenario after scenario.
I wanted to know
what I thought.

I was adding to my self-evaluation almost daily.
I would berate myself for saying something
or not saying something.

One poor guy was just shaking nervous when we met.
I told him to calm down,
I put my pants on
one long gorgeous leg at a time.

You can't make this stuff up!
How crazy is it that?
"I" would say something like that?

Since court was over,
I was very much suffering
from something like PTS
or something.

I just felt like I was not able
to take care of the house
the yard
pool
and weeds.

I know you might be thinking –
really sad.
I was working just to pay
for all this constant work.

My K's were moving on to AZ,

in another month.

Don's son drove by the house weekly at least.
He was not going to give up.

A friend sent me the newspaper clipping.
The ambulance chaser attorney was in the news.
His truck was being repo-ed
he shot at the tow truck guy.

He tried to tell the police
that he thought the guy
was stealing his truck.

Disbarred and incarcerated
end of story.

The court finally released my accounts
the house was mine officially,
I put it on the market.
It was appraised at 1.4 million.
Yeah!

The market had been great for sellers
when Don passed
but had tanked the last almost 2 years.
I got an offer for $740 K
yeah

I flew out to Colorado
to see one of my sons and his sweet family.
I was so happy
playing with my granddaughter
being a grandma.

They kept wanting me to go look at the model homes.
I walked down with my daughter in law.

The models were very nice.
I just didn't want all that house.
They were all 2 story houses.
I was thinking my next place would be a ranch style.

I looked at a house a few blocks from them.
I could just get on a plane
go places.
It was wild.

I still cried when I thought about Don.
I couldn't believe this
had been part of my life.

I tried to imagine his sons
tackling their dad
the joy they all would share.

What do I do?
This was the most terrifying decisions.

I know I do not make good decisions.
God help me, I'm truly paralyzed with fear.

PART 4

HIGH ELEVATION AND EXPECTATIONS...

I did the scariest thing,
I bought a house.
In Colorado! –

I've lived in California for 40 years.
My house in Colorado was in escrow,
I made it contingent on the sale of the California house.

The K's left one after the other
I tried to just be brave and smile
I had to turn around
walk into the house
because I just broke down.

I later learned it hurt my friend
that I didn't seem to care.
I do have far to go,
I am fearful of rejection
letting someone see what I'm feeling-
good, bad or indifferent.

It was a big shock moving
to a place where there are actual seasons.

Snow was the big one.
I didn't know I was supposed to shovel snow.
Nick came down and shoveled for me.

When I found out I had to drive in snow.
I was terrified.

If it was a heavy fog in California,
the road just shut down.
If there was ever snow.
No one would leave their home.
Driving in snow is scary as heck.
I had to wear layers and gloves too.

I've never worn layers – I get too hot!

The air is super thin, they say.
I thought I was having heart or lung problems.
That part gets better,
it takes a bit,
but it does get better.
I spent a lot of time with the kids.
Everyone together is great,
I miss the ones in California too.

I started attending the little church
that was meeting in the elementary school
right across from my house.

Seeing all the couples together in church,
holding hands and smiling at each other
made me miss Don so much more.

Dating had been a total bust in California.
I figured maybe I would meet someone
when the time was right.

I got a couple part times jobs
then applied at Macy's.
I got hired.

Turns out working at Macy's
is similar to owning a boat.
The best days are the day you Start (buy it)
the day you quit (sell it.)

I did not love it.
I sold shoes,
which is a commission position.
Sales was not my forte'
I stayed there until I found a new job.

I was so grown up.

DISTANT SIGHT FROM THE PAST

I started being a mentor for single moms at church.
I listened to these young moms
saying the things that I had said.

They expressed feelings that I had felt as well.
I was finally someplace where
I had some knowledge born of trials
that would be useful.

I told them when you are a mom
with 1 or 3 kids trying to keep your head
above water and your absent husband
or ex tells you he needs help.

You feel bad for him?
He asks for ½ your tax return
you consider it.

Your kids are saying poor daddy.
You don't want to take any money
from him because he is struggling.

He calls you heartless or worse
if you don't give in to his requests.

"That" is where you tell him
to suck it up go be a real man.

What a horrible example for his children.
Open your eyes and see how strong you are.
Trust God talk to other moms and encourage each other.
Sometimes the best way
to see how ridiculous a situation is,
is to hear someone
going through it being played.

Pray God opens your eyes

mends your heart.

Know it is alright
to take care of yourself
your family first.

I told them to take one class at a time
in the local college
they would find themselves with a degree
in no time at all.

We worked on skills that would
lead to good jobs
encouraged each one
to stay involved with bible studies.
Help other moms by being a sounding board.
We worked through a book called "Boundaries"
I needed this too.

I had times when I would make my 20-minute drive home,
that I wondered if I had said anything that would help these ladies.
I know whose voice that was.
I started to sing all the way home after each meeting.

I had joined Match.com.
I pretty much struck out with that.
It was my birthday
It was the last day of my subscription.
I posted that it had been interesting.
I hope you all find your soul mate.

I got a reply from a guy saying,
Happy Birthday.
I was so touched.
I said thank you, kind sir.
We chatted on the phone
I gave him my phone number,

so, we could talk some more.

We met in town to play volley ball at a church.
I met a bunch of folks that enjoyed getting together
once a week to have some fun.

He came out to pick me for dinner one night.
He called when he got to town,
"Are you East or
West of 60?"
I was trying to figure out where I was,
I don't know from east or west.

I wet my finger and held it up
I pulled some grass and threw it up in the air
I tried to see where the sun was
I tried to find my shadow

There was no East or West to be discovered by me.
Mountains are west,
how does that tell me if I'm West of 60?

He finally did make it to my house.

We went to a Mexican place
a little way down a road somewhere.

We got a table and ordered Margarita's.
We talked and laughed like crazy.
The young man that waited on us was new at his job.
He came over and ask if he could do anything for us.

I said, "Can you sing or dance?"
He was somewhat dumb struck,
"No" he finally said.

"Would you like for me to?"

I was acting like I was going to get up.
Kelly looked at the poor kid and said,
"She's kidding, I think"

The poor waiter laughed nervously and walked away quickly.

We talked about my late husband
turned out his late wife also.
Both had died of cancer.
We shared fun stories and heartbreaks too.

We enjoyed almost everything the same.
I told him one thing he needed to know is that
I don't cook breakfast.

The way we like the same stuff
I wouldn't know if I liked my eggs or not.
Best not to take a chance.

Turns out he'd rather have a
smothered green chili breakfast burrito.
He has a wit that just doesn't end.
Now I know how much
People must just love "my" humor.

Six months later, I called my mom
to tell her we were getting married
how excited I was.

I told her about the wedding gown
the colors and the reception ideas.
She said, "Ty Beth this is your third marriage
you are doing the whole church and dress thing?"

"Oh no, mom"
"It is my 4th marriage,
we would love for you to come if you want."

She didn't.

Love your enemy,
Ok I try to do this.
Today I am aware of a sad truth.
It is harder to continue to have affection
for a family member who is continually
harsh and unloving, then to love your enemy.

I have prayed on many occasions for her
she continues to be wicked to me,
I ask God to sauve whatever the cause of the hurt
that makes her strike out.
One who should be a beloved family member
who you should love
and should love you?

Do I have to love her anyway?
That just doesn't seem right,
it is so not fair!
God says to me in a small voice this morning,
"I love you, I forgive you,
I chose to forget all the times
you mistreated me and my family".

"Come be loved
let My love pour out of you,
when yours is all gone".

Its "Me" –
I am the one who needs forgiveness.
It's God's family,
the beloved family member is God's child.

I am God's child,
somehow the mystery of your mother
being your sister in Christ

is hard to wrap your head around.

I'm such a slow learner.
Thank you, God, for your patience.

Kelly and I hiked in Estes Park at lot.
My first hike with him was to Cub lake.
This particular day we hiked to Cub lake,
he wanted us to get down to the water's edge.

He pointed down the lake, "look at all those water lilies"
I looked it was beautiful,
"the reflection of the mountains In the water was looks ama-
When I turned back to him, he was on one knee.
The sun glinted off the diamond ring he held.

"Ty, will you marry me?"
Oh my gosh – I was crying
Yes, babe, Yes!
Geezalou! Where did you have the ring?
He laughed, "in my shirt pocket"

Kelly wanted to marry me
He asked me
He set a date
I never wondered what he was thinking.
He told me constantly,
I was about to be loved for the rest of my life.

We were married the beginning of the next year.
We wanted communion to be part of our ceremony.
We picked out songs
we worked through our choices
things to include in our ceremony
from a worksheet.

Our choices were identical

except for one question.
That question gave three choices
we both narrowed it to two
he picked one and I the other.

We got married in a church in
wedding clothes, with
wedding guests,
wedding pictures.
and every other detail for the perfect wedding.

He even got a limousine
to take us to the wedding reception.
The whole family came out
it was a dream come try.

We got to the Wedding Suite
he gave me a Valentine's bracelet
and chocolate dipped strawberries.

The wedding of my dreams.
We celebrate our Vala-Versary every year.

Our two young granddaughters
were the flower girls.
Haley was in most of our pictures
and our dances too.

I think the best thing
I ever got her was papa.

Grace was great in our pictures,
but she was happy to just watch the action.

A grandma's dream wedding
would certainly include
a "Candy Bar"

Everyone got a polka dotted bag
that had our names and wedding date.
There was a big round table
with candy in different jars and bowls.
They could fill their bags
as much as they wanted.

I loved the wonder and smiles.

Our cake was two layers,
my layer had a crystal Cinderella carriage and horses,
his layer was off to the side
overlapping mine it had a crystal semi-truck.
The statue of him was
reaching down to pull me up
mine was reaching up.
Kelly celebrates me,
he says he loves me countless times a day.
If he turns over in the night he says,
I love you.
Now almost 10 years later,
we have 9 kids and spouses,
who we love
and 17 grandkids too.

We love every one of them
they love us too.
We are a tight family
excited to see and spend time always.

I got "my gift" just when I needed him.
He has been my rock.
He can settle me down and
cheer me up.

He can just listen
let me be totally stupid,

until I figure out
that's what I'm doing.

He gets my crazy humor
can battle me quip for quip
like no one ever has been able to do.
I have never felt so loved.
I can do whatever I want,
he will support me the whole way.

One of our Val-versaries,
Kelly gave me one of the bests gifts
he's ever given me.

A gift certificate for one of those
wine and painting classes.
I went to the class
I got the bug!

I decided I could do this cheaper at home
any time I want.
I started painting in 2011.

God has blessed my efforts,
I have gotten better and better.
People actually want my paintings.

I do know why artists get famous after they're dead.
I don't have confidence in my abilities.
As far as what art critics may say, who knows.
I love to create,
it calls me sometimes in the middle of the night.

I might go into my "studio"
Saturday morning early
Only to have Kelly call
down to ask me if I wanted dinner.

Remembering my place…

####################

Oh, thank you Lord
for our many blessings.
How many times have I prayed this?

Nice house, good food, beautiful yard, new truck, so much stuff.

Blessings?
Sure, these things are good,
but is this what we pray about?
I am truly burdened
with the substance of my prayers.

Father please give me
strength
courage
and guide me to be your hands and feet.

Give me a heart for service
and feet for service.
Equip me through your Word,
fight for me Lord
against the powers that would
hold me comfortable,

In the nice house
the nice yard
the air conditioning.

My heart breaks
for the hurt it must be for you
to see me in comfort
wishing that everyone else
was blessed with comfort.
Father the more I step out
the more I have hardship

and discomfort,
that is how I know-

I am going in the right direction.

Today afresh I put on the full armor of God.
Eph. 6:14-17
14.Stand firm then, with the belt of truth buckled around your waist,
with the breastplate of righteousness in place,
15. and with your feet fitted with the readiness that comes from the
gospel of peace.
16. In addition to all this, take up the shield of faith, with which you
can extinguish all the flaming arrows of the evil one.
17. Take the helmet of salvation and the sword of the Spirit, which is
the word of God.

Forgive me Father for not using the tools that you have so
graciously provided.
This is the true blessing,
that each day is new,
your blessings are fresh again.
I love you Lord.

###################

THINKING PRAYERFULLY

Fresh off a big blessing this morning,
God answered prayer
that I was told was a wasted effort.

What a thrill to enlist the prayers warriors
see the mighty results.
God honors those who honor Him!

I am so often surprised
by the way God
works out the impossible.

As a follower of the Lord Jesus Christ –
We are "Representatives" of Christ!
We are Re – presenting our Savior.
As Christians we are
sending messages all the time.

Sometimes Intentionally
sometimes unintentionally.
What does that mean?
People who are in need of salvation
frequently only realize it
when they see a life
being lived Gracefully,
Prayerfully,
Mercifully,
Generously,
Humbly
and Honestly.

By doing this
our actions are our witness
we have no need
to defend ourselves and
detract from our witness.

If we can train ourselves
to see an angry person
as someone hurting
feeling as though
they have no control
or are not getting their way,
it can give us pause
to show compassion.

Remember "a kind word turns away wrath" –
the unexpected act of grace
soon disarms anger and fear also.
What is that saying?
"Be graceful when the unexpected happens."
 – by being unexpected,
Grace abounds.

THOUGHTS OF MOM..

534

Wanting and needing your parent,
spouse or child
to affirm love and connection is normal.

I wanted to have a bond
with my mother
my whole life.

I called her every time
I was in need of
comfort
love
or to share joy.

Over and over
all my years.
She just had nothing to offer.

Each of my siblings
had times of "In"
with our mother,

Each one would take such joy
in the time of approval
live in that moment
as though it would never end.

The four of us girls
would honor the one
who was in the,
what to call it?

It was like one was let inside the force field.

One thing we could always count on
was the in would become the out once again.

Always the outing,
was accomplished with
great drama
and stinging hurtful language.

The scene was as one might expect
from someone who stumbles
upon an intruder most hideous.
-how did you ever get in?
The boys were pretty much always out.

I had stopped being part of this sadness.
I didn't try to get in
or let her keep me out.
I just was and so was she.

SHINE LIGHT ON THE DARKNESS

Mom had to have back surgery.
The doctor told her
she had to stop smoking
she would not heal.

She stopped
for two days
before the surgery.

She had COPD
had to be on oxygen.
Which she still used
while she smoked.

She finally did quit smoking
somehow.
She started using the Vape things.
She coughed so bad
that she was constantly wet.
What torment
to lose control of bodily functions.
She spent her time
alone in her senior living apartment.

She got real sick
had to go to the hospital.
She had pneumonia.

The doctor thought the vapor was introducing
way too much moisture into her lungs.

Faith ended up taking her home
to stay with her.
She got some better
but not completely.

About 2-3 weeks later,

I got a call from my sister
to tell me mom was sick.

My sisters were at the hospital with her.
The doctor thought the pneumonia was back.
He said they had a difficult time
seeing her lungs
with whatever they were using.

He decided to try an x-ray.
Finally, they were informed
that after x-rays they had discovered
the whole back half of
mom's heart was –

black and dead.

I had no reaction.
Just stunned.

Days later Faith found mom in the morning.
She had passed in the night.
Where will our mother be?

She was a tormented soul her whole life.

Did she really know Jesus?
I hope she did,
while none of us deserve heaven,
it hurts to think she went anywhere else.
I just keep thinking,
"you will know them by their fruits,
they will have love among themselves."

The funeral service was oddly uncomfortable,
all of us kids were there together.
I had thoughts of dad's funeral,

which broke my heart.
I don't quite feel that now.

My little brother said he really didn't have any feelings.
He said he would not
stand up and say nice things about her.
I told him we had all mourned the loss
of our mother our whole lives.
Those were his exact words at the funeral.

Only one sister cried
and said how she loved our mom
and how wonderful mom was.

Two other sisters had been
either yelled at or shunned
days prior to mom's death.

My little sister said she wanted to hold moms hand
tell her she loved her
have her say it back,
she didn't go to her.
She was afraid
mom would not say it back.

We each stood up to say something about our mom.
One said, mom said to always look your best.
Another said mom was talented.

I stood up and said,
"I'm the pretty one"
I had wizard of oz in my head.
I said she had taught me to cook,
clean, and sew.

Most of us didn't say,
I loved her,

or she loved me.

A couple of the grandkids
said how sad they were.
She had had a relationship with
 a couple of the great grand kids,
that was like a grandma.

Friends of hers
from the area said how much fun she was
how she was always so generous
how talented she was.
They each said they would miss her very much.

SORTING THE JEWELS..

We got together at our sister's house.
We ate left over food from the funeral.
My sister wanted me to come
pick something out of mom's jewelry case.
I told her no thank you
several times.

She said all the rest of us
have picked something.

I walked into my sister's bedroom
looked at the jewelry cabinet
I had given mom years before.

I raised the lid and just stood there.
My sister said, "what about these?"
"Some earrings",
I found a pair of pearl earrings,

"I like these if no one else wants them."
"Take them" she said.

"Those are the ones mom had on when she died."

Of course, I can't get that out of my mind.
So many times,
in this life
mom and I had picked
the same thing out
in the same color.

I found myself once again
pondering what had made two people
that had so many similar tastes
be unable to have a loving relationship.
I wear those pearls a lot.

What was at the edge of my mind...

Mother has been gone now several months.
Mother's Day will be in two days.
This year I won't
go stand in
the card isle
of some store
to find a card
a card that would convey,
honor and thoughtfulness
while not adding syrupy
mother Teresa-esk, lies.

Had I honored my mother?

The weather has gotten warmer,
only to be told we will have
Snow for Mother's Day.

Not a huge deal.
Just when I think my membership,
in the surgery of the month club
has finally expired.

I am two weeks post-surgery
for a major southern movement
of all my plumbing.
It has been a slow recovery.

What does one do
when you must stay very low activity.
I really wanted to go pull weeds,
can't go pull weeds.
I really wanted to organize drawers and closets,
couldn't really do that.

Even sweeping, mopping, and vacuuming are painful,
ok I tried to do that.

In the end,
I prayed a lot.
I got off into long talks with God.

We talked about prayers
that were almost answered,
and I gave up too soon.
Prayers were answered,
and miraculously

I had given up
my trust in God,
just before the answer came.

Times where I managed to offer
a good word to someone hurting.
Situations that I figured out
what would have been the best idea.

We talked about how many times
I had run full bore
into something I wanted
before I realized
I had forgotten to talk to Him.

I am consumed with
an undefinable something.
I can't put a face to the issue
that is forefront in my mind.

I was not settled with my mother gone.
I thought it would end.
What is it?

I sit and contemplate the loss.
It is not losing her
but that of the loss of possibility
for some sort of reconciliation.

Our time was what it was,
that has ended now.

That bond, cannot this side of heaven, be.
Why is it so difficult to let it go?
It has been two years since my mother passed away.

My sisters frequently post on Facebook,
of missing her.
I don't miss who she was here.
I hope for who she is now.
I do spend lots of time
of introspection.

I want to know that my children
have a good mother
that I am doing all that I can
to see that they are equipped
for every good work.

They each felt
the terrible loss of Don
I'm sure they are forever changed.

My new daughters and sons
have each grown me
with very different thoughts and ideas.

They need and want me to varying degrees.
They encourage me as much as I do them.
They lost their mother to cancer
almost 20 years ago now.

They have a different appreciation for a mother's love.
They understand loss very intimately.
They fill a need in me that they can't possibly understand.
I feel an impossible blood tie with them.

In no small way,
my 9 children and
17 grandchildren
are my undeserved gift.

I am fully theirs to whatever degree
they want
or need me
as long as I live.

#####################

Today I attended the funeral of a very sweet lady.
She had written letters to those of us left behind.
Some individuals and some en masse.

The theme Love your brothers and sisters.
Offer encouraging words
be ever ready to forgive.
Tell those you love
that you love them.

This was the fourth funeral in a month.
It just puts one to thinking
those things that need to be arranged for,
hopefully some day after, say your 95th birthday.

What songs to play –
What stories to tell –
even what to do with this earthly shell.

I know,
first, I need to be concerned with
going about the Father's work.
He invites us all to share in the harvest.

Follow His leading and increase the kingdom.
Do I do this all the time? No.
Do I want to? YES

When we fail to ask God
or to thank God
for our daily needs and blessings,
it is likened to a spoiled child
that feels he in entitled to whatever he wants.

I'll work on this.
My project is to make my visits
to the fountain of regret,
fewer and farther between.

I pray for wisdom over and over
I am slowly getting more and more.
Emphasis on "Slowly".

I guess my point today is –
Keep living, until you die.
Leave the remembrance to those left behind.
Work on what they will remember.

Again, I must reiterate,
I would like better attendance to my funeral
then I've had
for my Tupperware parties.

Just say'n

####################

MY FATHER

I have not had any contact with my father
since I was 17 years old.
My two brothers have taken turns
over the last few years
helping take care of our father
as he is having more and more
difficulty taking care of himself.

It is the middle of Oct 2015 –
I got news that my father
had had a massive stroke.

This news filled me with
indescribable foreboding.

I walked around for a few minutes.
I was running a diagnostic on me.
Do I have any feelings?
I am feeling something, what is it?

I have learned to stop my feelings
hold them in check with traumatic things
so much that they do it on their own now.

Is my father going to hell?
Tears filled my eyes.
Tears forded my stoic lids
cascaded waterfall-esk.

Within moments I was overcome.
God please I don't want my father to go to hell.
Father, has he asked for your forgiveness?

Please father don't let him die
without the chance to repent.
Father in my selfishness

I want to see him in heaven
to be able to feel the love of my father
as you intended.
I have done so many things in my life
that don't deserve your forgiveness,
yet though your Son I am saved and redeemed.

I forgive him,
I plead that he can still
hear your voice and say, Yes!

I called my brother.
Rudy told me our father was paralyzed
one whole side of his body,
couldn't talk and didn't recognized
our little brother
who was there with him.

My older brother had been one of our father's victims too,
He stayed in touch and kept a relationship
with our dad throughout his life.

I just could not.
Neither of us attempted to dissuade the other
in any way to their side.
When I called my brother back
to get an update
he asked why I cared,
not in a mean way, just surprised.

I don't want him to go to hell.
I don't know if he has ever repented
and taken Jesus as his savior.
"Oh sis",
"When I would go to see him on Sundays,
he always had his church shows on,
he had his bible all noted up." I cried.

"I don't have any good memories of him,
ever"
"Me neither sis"
"I think Randy does,
dad took him fishing and stuff"

I was relieved that Randy
didn't have experiences
we had had.

"Will you tell Randy I love him,
keep me informed?"
"I will sis,
I love you"
"I love you to brudder,"

I texted, my pastor.
I asked for prayer
and filled him in,
the message went out
to the prayer chain.

I called to get an update
they said our father was awake
moving around in his bed.

I prayed some more
and cried.
I sat in a chair and watched tv
for 3 hours
just, so I couldn't think.
I prayed that night again
and felt a peace.

When I got up my phone
had a text from my brother that said,
"Dad is up walking around"

– I texted back –
OMG Thank God!!

I don't know what
this means in any other way.
I have peace

I feel that there is Hope.
The evidence of a redeemed life
is at least present.
That is what I shall rest in.

Our father has advanced dementia.
He may have seen the last of us in this life.
He will battle this cruel fate
until his end on this earth.

God is faithful.
I can't help but to think
my loving heavenly father
allowed this for "me".

In church, we have talked many times
recently about people being hurt
in their lives.

Children being abused
has also been in the conversation.
People say this is the worst
possible horror that could ever be.
That this is the most unforgivable act.

I believe any time a person,
child or otherwise is torn down
with evil language
or action it is equally terrible,
but none are unforgivable.

God's Son died
for ALL sin,
and sinners.

Dad had a stroke in the night
a week or so later.

My little brother brought him back to Atascadero
for the funeral.
Rudy and I both flew out.
Kelly & Betty of course came with us.

We went to the viewing
I did not want to look at him.
At the funeral the next day
there was a letter about Jim,
in the vestibule.

It listed his military service,
and family, I was not listed.
There was also a little clipping from a magazine.
He wrote articles for a magazine.

I was so angry I almost had to leave.
I did not want to share writing with him.
I did not want to inherit anything from him.

Kelly kept me together
we went in to the chapel and sat down.

Randy was concerned that I might
make a scene, without reason.

I just wanted to see that it was all real.
People stood up to say how wonderful he was
what an influence he had been in their lives.
I was squeezing Kelly's leg

I hadn't even realized it.

After the service
I was trying to just catch my breath.
Rudy went up and told the Pastor
that he just needed to know
that all the nice things those people said
were for someone we didn't know.

He told him that man, pointing to Jim,
that man was a monster
to me and my sister
who knows who else.

He just needed to finally
say it out loud.
Rudy came straight to me
and told me what he had done.

I was surprised because he never seemed
affected by our child hood.
He too had learned to cope.

My surprise with my feelings at seeing him
being around him cannot be voiced.
After the weeks prior of despair,
I couldn't make any of it
fit into any sort of sense

PART 5

CHRISTMAS EVE

We have waited all year to get to spend Christmas,
with the kids.
Final preparation for their visit has been made.

It is snowy and cold,
we don't mind that at all.
We have games, snacks and
fun for all.

Off we go to church in a few moments.
Last look at my notes and we are ready.
Kelly has the prayer to begin service
I have the devotional before communion.

He prayed before two Christmas Eve services,
words of faith from his heart, spilled out like water.

I think it was God's heart that came though.
He said how tiny he felt
when he looked into the vast skies of Colorado.

How humbled he was to know God loves him.
He thanked Jesus for coming into the world
even though it was going to be to a terrible death
on the cross, to bring us redemption.
He prayed that we would all accept that gift
Jesus came to bring to each one individually.

His voice cracked as he choked up,
I reached out and touched him,
prayed for him,
I thanked God for the gift this man is to me.

I gave the devotional before communion,
It is rather scary to talk before the whole church,
but I love the opportunity to do so.

When I signed up for Dec 24th for some reason
it didn't mean Christmas eve to me.

I know and feel known
by all those in our little church,
it's easier to talk to, "Family".

We were of course talking about
the birth of baby Jesus coming to save the world.
I decided to talk about babies.
I wrestled with the way to make this point
and to make it memorable.

As we've already established,
I have a God given sense of humor.
I have a need to use it for Him when I can.

I took the microphone and stood up.
We sit in a circle around the Lord's table,
I walked around the circle
so that I could face everyone as I told my story.

I ask, while raising my hand in the air,
"Who here had a baby,
parented a baby or
was presently a baby?" (laughter)

So, I began,
we know it goes something like this.

Food in, food out,
Cry, sleep. Cry, Food out, food in,
Cry, sleep, cry, food out,
Oops out some more,
cry, cry some more.

And then, sometimes

"the baby cries too!"

How would a baby come to save us?
I felt I needed to be saved from
the baby on more than one occasion.

This morning we need to answer a couple questions about –
"wise men" – Kings? wealthy men? 3 or more?

They had to have an entourage, kings and wealthy men
didn't strike out on 40-day jaunts by themselves
(it took them 40 days to get to the baby form Herod's palace.

Who knows from where they originated,
there's a lot of East from Bethlehem, I've heard)
at a time when thieves and robbers were everywhere
they had to have guards and servants.
We really don't know all those details,
but God saw fit to give us enough to see His plan.

God sent his only son
that he might redeem the world
from sin and restore us to Him.

We remember
his birth,
his life,
his death on a cross,
and most importantly his Resurrection.

We share in communion as a reminder
until he comes back again as he promised.
We drink of the juice that represents Jesus blood shed for us.
We eat the bread that represents his body broken for us.
I invite you to partake communion as a family.

I made it through two services
the devotional was fairly close to the same both times.

How did I ever end up being someone
a pastor would trust
with a microphone
and a story?

This life of mistakes,
some multiple times,
on my side.

But God doesn't make mistakes.
I imagine how others see me,
but really who knows how others see,
it's taken me many, many years
to see myself even slightly
as God does.

I can now forgive my mistakes,
make fewer mistakes
and forgive others who can't forgive me.
Old Fashioned Christmas

The kids will arrive sometime soon.
The memories will take shape and the
time will fly by.
Then they will be gone again,
In the blink of an eye.

The house was full of people.
I had planned games and food.
I wrapped the gifts as Breckin,
had delivered for 3 weeks prior.
The tree was beautiful and packed with boxes.

I told the kids it was grandma house rules –

Eat whatever you want
Whenever you want.
Where ever you want.

We worked a puzzle that was just the
outlines of the picture.
You had to color it
after it was completed it
We finished it about 3 days later.

They decorated the faux, (graham crackers)
ginger bread houses.
All 6 were exceptional.
Ages from 5- 17.
Very imaginative too.

They gave us unending hugs
we laughed and laughed.
I read them a Christmas story,
they all came over and sat with me
and listened to every word.

They made several trips to the hot tub
of course, they had to tromp through
the snow for that. They didn't care.
I wanted all kinds of good memories for them.
They gave me all kinds of memories instead,
or maybe also.

SAFE TRIP..

The kids were heading back to Texas.
3am is way too early to get up in the morning.
Still I'm barely up and got my robe on and hair combed.
I'm just glad I wasn't the one to "get to"
get 6 kids up and going this morning.
Breckin is a most fetching red head.

She has the best smile
and loves her kids to the moon.
She brought each kiddo up,
sent them to the bathroom.
She ran through a mental list
confirmed each one had their electronic devices.

Then off to the next one.
Grace was last.
Grace is a tall,
dark haired beauty,
with a smile to rival her mom's.

She had on shorts a hoody and boots,
her pillow and phone in her hand
her back pack hanging from her arm.

"There is snow on the ground", I said.
"I just have to go to the car grandma,
I'll be fine" she gave me an early morning half smile.
I hugged her to me and told her I loved her,
she hugged me back and said she loved me to.

I gathered them all into my arms,
no small feat.
"I love you all so much,
Thank you for playing all the games
decorating the ginger bread houses,
you can't imagine how much it means to me"

In almost unison they said,
"we loved it grandma, it was so fun."
"I can't wait until your back this summer"
"We'll get to go do some hiking or something" Hugs again.

Luis had started the SUV
was arranging the belongings of 5 boys
and the Christmas bounty for the trip home.
Six beautiful grandkids were here most of the week
you would hardly believe it.

Now the pile of shoes by the door was almost gone.
One last run through for electronics cords and lost socks.
Hugs were handed out
sweet little voices saying I love you grandma.
Grandpa got them right after I did.
Breckin hugged me so tight and I hugged her tight to.
"We will see you in June,"
"I love you so much"
"I love you too"

Luis stepped in the door blowing in to his gloves.
"ok, do we have everything?"
"Get over here in our group hug"
"I'm coming" he pushed in.

Kelly said, "Let me pray over you"
He was praying,
I was listening, but I was beaming too.
I love that man so much.
We have both grown so much over the last few years.

We both have loved our little church
And our pastor so very much.
It's not the people
or the pastor either.

It's God working here,
we are here to be part of His work.
A pastor that listens to the Lord
instills into all those who will listen
and hear the truth that we all need
to be equipped for good works.

A Christmas from the past
with all the wonder of years gone by...

What a blessing they are to me.
I love those babies so much.
Babies, that's funny.

Grace will graduate from high school
this year and off to college.
One last kiss and out the door.
We watched and waved as they
backed out of the driveway,
then off down the snowy street.

I am still so happy from such a memorable holiday.
I walked myself back through the house
plopped right back in bed.
One more quick prayer
for their safe trip home
and I was back to sleep.

RELISHING THE MEMORIES

When I woke again, I needed coffee and creamer.
To tell the truth,
I like a little coffee in my creamer.
I am standing here with the fridge door open,
I had filled up it up with everything
I could think of and the little fridge with small sodas.

We worked hard making candy and goodies
for the last 2 weeks getting ready for them to arrive.
They did a good job of helping us
get rid of all those sweets, such troopers.

I love being a grandma so much.
How in the world could
God make being a grandparent
even better than being a parent?

I just want all my kids and grandkids to know
how special and loved they are.

Colorado Travis super enjoyed cooking
and trying new recipes,
if he says that's not true –
he's fibbing.

He makes Cheesecake from scratch
in my 12-year-old springform pan
that I have never used!
He is one of my boys for sure,
I love him to the full moon and back, wait –

I think that's a full moon?

I was a little disappointed not to get the WAM Fam
but Nick & Amy decided the "inn" would be too full.
I'm sure we will see them sometime in the new year.

Nick sent a picture of Henry
finally getting his long red curls cut off.
I guess 3rd grade makes you really grow up.
I was looking forward to Hailey playing her ukulele for us.
Miss Lily my joy, has the best stories
she is the cuties little spitfire ever.

Rocky and Mishka might not have hit it off
in these tight quarters,
never know what grand dogs will do.

I just wish I could spend more time
with each one of the kids and the grandkids too.
I would always love a lot of them under the same roof ,a lot.

Megan must value that too,
she is the best hostess
she loves family around a lot also.

Travis is home to get a running start
on his college loans and general debt.

Being a single person at this time of the world
makes it difficult to become a homeowner.
It has been much smoother than I expected,
considering he brought a 90-pound pit bull with him.

I have never been a big fan of dogs and dogs
in the house
Not a fan at all.

She rescued Travis,
at a shelter in Utah.
His job sent him there for a couple years,
she saved him from missing the rest of us too much.

Mishka is her name

she is an adult and looks very scary
when she comes running up with her teeth showing until,
you realize she is grinning.
She would love to be a lap dog if she could be.
I find that I love her,
Hair of the dog soothes what ails you
after all.

HOME IS MORE THAN AN ADDRESS..

The weather is cooler this morning.
I sit by the window with my bible in my hands
scanning this verse and that.
What do you have for me this day Lord?
I don't want to play bible roulette –
open the book and put my finger blindly on a verse –
and just know God led me there.
Not so much.

I have had many
days lately that I opened my bible
felt the urge to place my hand on it
close my eyes and wait.

So, I do,
I am overcome with the compulsion
to search my mind for passages
that I have tucked away.

I know God is Faithful,
just, yet merciful,
and patient.

I can scan my minds files
pull out all kinds of truths.
I can't tell you every address,
but they weren't written with addresses.

I think knowing the book
hiding its truths in my heart
are enough.

I have comfort and assurance
that through God's son Jesus
made a way for me.
That's in His Book.

I want my house to be a happy
And loving place.

I've got a lot of bedrooms to have lots of guests.
I have guest rooms in my house.
I am so thrilled and excited to have family come.

I prepare their rooms
with love and anticipation
for those I love to be comfortable
and pampered.

Fresh sheets for the bed.
Fragrant soaps for the bathroom.
Soft thick towels.
Even flowers.

For those who have gone to sleep in the Lord
have gone on to their room prepared in the Father's house.

Is it in a much grander scale, very similar?
I have so much love for my short time guest,
but the Father has infinitely more Love.
For, those whose rooms He has readied,
are not guests but have come home

THINGS OF VALUE...

I can cook and bake
it feels like I've been cooking
my whole life, at least it seems like it.
Cooking makes people happy.
Maybe it's eating that makes people happy,

Can't really have one without the other.
Cooking and eating I mean.

Happiness, happiness can be found in many things
or can be found in nothing.
Happiness that doesn't come from God
isn't happiness at all, but a sheer wisp of smoke.
Gone as soon as the next thing comes along.

Real happiness – "Joy" that comes from God,
Is present and real even when circumstances
don't reasonably expect it.

We have so many moments of pride,
protection, success
failure and trials
with this amazing family.

Looking back at situations
that looked most bleak,
only to see God was working.
Trusting Him when things are tough is hard
but trusting Him when things
appear hopeless,
is accelerating!

Times, I had no idea what to say
He worked it out.
I usually stay ~~strong~~ faithful almost to the end
and then blow it.

Yes, I am a Bible character.
They screwed up left and right,
silly humans.
God used it all.
I will keep trying, always.